The Secret Life of a Housewife

by Linda Howard

Logos International
Plainfield, New Jersey

To
Frank
Mark, Leah and Carol

The Secret Life of a Housewife
Copyright © 1978 by Logos International
All rights reserved
Printed in the United States of America
Library of Congress Catalog Card Number: 78-60946
International Standard Book Number: 0-88270-296-3
Published by Logos International, Plainfield, New Jersey 07060

Table of Contents

1

The Secret Life of a Housewife

My grocery cart squeaked and jerked into the check-out line. I stooped to pick up the orange juice which had fallen again from the top of my piled heap of frozen and packaged foods.

An imbalanced wheel on the too-small buggy made the final leg of my grocery trip miserable. The cart was impossible to guide and the orange juice took periodic bounces onto the floor.

As I bent over unloading the groceries, another shopper pranced by. Every nail was polished, even her hair was combed. Her cart was loaded in neat stacks. Each stack was obviously cataloged according to a complex color code. All the red foods were in the back right hand corner, all the greens in the front, etc.

I turned my head away from my neighbor's cart with envy. The memory of a girl I met in high school crossed my mind. Her name was Becky Swicegood.

Becky was a straight A student, beautiful, discreet, and

polite. She never suffered from S.S. (Your slip's showing.) Her perfection went so far that she always had a folded Kleenex in her purse whenever I had to blow my nose. She didn't use Kleenex because, naturally, she was not a public nose blower.

The thing which always frustrated me about Becky was that I knew that hidden deep within my breast I was capable of that kind of perfection. But, somehow, I always chose the cart with a squeaky, imbalanced wheel.

The Master of Metamorphosis, however, is busy changing me. I realize I'm like a caterpillar who has spun a cocoon of protection around myself. The cocoon keeps out hurt, harm and rain but it has also kept out the sunlight and love. But slowly, something is changing.

I'm becoming a being of flight and grace, a butterfly. The real Linda Howard will one day emerge. Not a gangling housewife with a squeaky wheel but a princess in God's kingdom.

Maybe then, I'll have color coded grocery stacks or at least a few folded tissues in case someone else has to blow their nose.

2

Runaway Housewives

The muffled, male voice on the other end of the phone was familiar, "Linda, can I speak to Frank?" The words shook with emotion.

Frank and I had been lying in bed talking and relaxing. I handed the receiver to him.

The conversation was lengthy. Frank was moved with a sense of grief that left him without words. He only groaned to the man on the other end of the phone. Finally, the conversation was over.

"That was Michael. Joyce has left him and the girls. He isn't sure where she is. He doesn't think another man is involved. She just left."

The shock waves pierced my heart and spirit as Frank continued his story. Michael and Joyce had been our friends for many years. Their two daughters were like our own children. Even though we moved from their hometown almost ten years ago, we've kept close contact with them.

It seemed that the pressure of being a wife and mother had

gotten to be too much. One night, Joyce appeared in the doorway with her bags packed and calmly announced that she was leaving. She had made arrangements for a woman to come in to take care of the girls in the afternoon after school. Michael would have to shoulder the responsibility the rest of the time. With little explanation, Joyce sighed, "I can't take it any more," and walked out.

I knew that this scene was being repeated many times over in thousands of American homes, yet that didn't relieve the sense of hurt we felt for our friends.

Someone has said that you can prove anything with a survey. Even though you can't put a great deal of stock in what this or that survey may reveal, you must be impressed by one which was taken during 1975. In that year there were more housewives who left home than teenagers.

Many of these women are like my friend. They leave children and husbands. There is no crisis, no final argument, no crushing blow. They just leave.

The pressures on the American housewife throw us into constant turmoil. We try to conform to all the standards of behavior set up by society. We should entertain like Pearl Mesta, cook like the Galloping Gourmet, sew like Debbie Reynolds, look like Farrah Fawcett-Majors, keep house like the television commercials and still have time for our children.

Being a Christian only adds to the pressure. Now we must add a mask of piety and church activities.

God, however, is not impressed with masks. He is interested in being sure that we have a right relationship with Him. If that means that He has to pull all the props out of our lives then He will pull them out.

The Christian housewife can never perform to the

perfection that the world and others expect. I have found that as I pull off my masks and say to the world, God and especially myself, "This is my problem. I can't cope in this area," a wonderful thing happens. God, through His Son Jesus, begins to pick up the pieces. In practical ways, He forgives, forgets and redeems.

Many times I've been like Joyce. I've cried, "Oh, God, I can't take it any more." And just as many times God has placed His tender and loving arms around me and said, "I know you can't cope, but I can." Then He begins to pry my tightly clenched fists away from the problem and He takes it.

Where can we run—we runaway housewives? Really, only to Jesus. No one else has the word of eternal life.

3

How Can I Leave Myself?

Ms. Moniger was tall, slender and impeccably dressed. The television host who was interviewing her had begun to probe the circumstances of her divorce.

"The thing which startled me," said Ms. Moniger, "was that after my divorce, nothing was settled. You see, I found that in many ways I was in worse condition. Before I had wanted to get out of marriage, I wanted out of the whole housewife scene. I got my wish. I found a job. It was rewarding, satisfying and paid well; but I saw that I had the same problems, the same frustration. There's no place else to go now. How can I leave myself?"

A friend in a nearby town expressed another problem one day as we sat having a sandwich. Because she is a Christian, her focus was different from Ms. Moniger.

"I wanted a ministry," Jane said smiling. Then suddenly tears formed in her eyes. "Linda, people don't seem to understand. God spoke to me in an audible voice. He told me I was to have a miracle ministry. Now everything has fallen apart. I'm so miserable."

I took my friend's shaking hand as she continued, "When we moved to this city, all I wanted was to be the best wife and mother I could. Then, the Lord spoke to me. It wasn't a quiet, still voice in my heart. It was audible. His presence filled the room. I have never felt such waves of love and peace in my life.

"I told the Lord I would give up everything for Him. I set out on my goal with a fury that would shame Peter. I let nothing stand in my way. Since then, my home has been a wreck. My husband left me. My children have all gone their way into the world."

Then just as quickly as the tears had appeared, a huge, winning smile spread across her face. Jane dabbed her eyes with her napkin, "I am going to have my ministry though. I don't care what my husband says. I don't care what anyone says. God promised me and I am going to follow through."

After lunch I had to rush to pick up my children from school. The car was quiet as I weaved my way toward the children. I began to put together the two scenes.

Ms. Moniger, the successful business woman. Jane with her ministry. I could understand both positions. I knew the frustrations of being "just a housewife." I also knew that from my earliest remembrances God had placed a call on my life.

"Lord," I prayed, my voice piercing the silence, "how can a woman mesh the two worlds together. Can she have a call on her life and still remain the kind of wife and mother she should be?"

Ignoring my question, the Lord got to the heart of the problem. "Linda," He spoke to my heart, "what is it you really want out of life?"

What did I really want? What were my deepest and most

8

lasting desires? Basically, it was an easy question. "Lord, more than anything I want to minister your love to my husband and children. I want to be a Christian housewife."

Paul the apostle gave some good sage advice to young women. He said that usually it was better for us to marry and have children. He implied that it was better not only for us but for society as well.

That day in the silence of my car the Lord settled once again what my priorities must be. My greatest call should always be to share the Lord with my family. I knew that any other ministry must come second. My first responsibility will be to my home.

4

Catch the Foxes

There are many things I've learned in the years I've been a housewife. A few of them are important, most of them are of little significance to anyone except the Lord and me. However, one thing stands out as monumental.

No matter how perplexing the problem or frustrating the situation, God can teach His love for me through that problem. I cannot always identify with the things my friends are being led through, but I deeply and painfully identify with all my own hurts and pains.

For the housewife it isn't the large looming crisis which tears and destroys our joy and peace. In the Song of Solomon the maiden, who must have been a housewife, tells the king, "The little foxes have come in and spoiled my vines." Those foxes were the little cubs which ate the grape plants before they could become nourished and bloom. The tender, light green shoots were eaten and destroyed by those little pests.

How often I have cried to my King, "Maybe I could trust you in the important crises, but what about today? What about this dull, boring routine I have to live in?" My prayer usually ends like the maiden in the Scripture. "Oh, God, catch the little foxes. Look! See how they've come in and spoiled my vineyard."

God has never left me in my state of frustration. He has never left me permanently perplexed. Each time He has lovingly looked down and lifted me up from my sea of unvacuumed carpets and dusty tables to catch the foxes and teach me how to replant my vines.

5

The Two Years
I've Spent Wiping
The Table

The other day in a fit of self-pity I decided to see how much of my life has been taken up wiping the table.

I tried in fairness to use conservative estimates. I figured that I wiped the table at least five times a day. It takes three minutes a wipe.

That is a most conservative estimation considering I have to find the dishrag each time. I can never tell where my rag may be found. I have narrowed it down to three probable possibilities though. It could be in the dog dish, outside near my son's surfboard or in one of the bedrooms.

Then I have to find the detergent. That's easier. It's almost always in the bathroom where one of the girls has used it to wash her hair or take a bubble bath.

Using these figures, I found that I have spent two working years of my married life wiping that table. That is an eight hour day, seven days a week, no vacations, no coffee breaks.

Do you realize what I could have done in these two years? I could have completed an associate's degree in education. I could have become a piano virtuoso. I could have completely wallpapered the house five times. I could have memorized the entire book of Romans in the Bible. I could have gotten the most wonderful tan at the beach anyone has ever seen.

I'm not sure what I'll do with this invaluable morsel of information. It would have made a wonderful toast someday. "Here's to the two years I've spent wiping the table." But I almost never make any toasts since we're complete teetotalers. It would look great on my epitaph though. It could simply read, "She spent two years wiping the table."

No. I think I'll begin to really put that time to work for me. In the future I could utilize the well-publicized practice of President and Mrs. Carter. When they read their Bibles each day, they use a Spanish-English edition. That way they are practicing their Spanish and learning God's Word at the same time.

Since I now know how much time is taken doing this simple task, I can use those moments for prayer. Each time I wipe the table I can pray for a sick friend or loved one. I can become a vital part of a ministry overseas by lifting a missionary up to the Father with every swipe.

Last year when Carol entered kindergarten, she was in a car pool. Toward the end of the year the car pool dissolved and I had to take Carol each day myself. The five minutes we rode to school were set aside for memorizing Scripture.

We were amazed to realize that we could learn two verses a week. In less than six weeks she had learned several chapters and most of the key Scriptures that point the way to Jesus as our Savior.

I also learned something about redeeming or buying back time. A few moments can become important blocks of time when they are put together over the years.

The Two Years I've Spent Wiping the Table

Wasted time, wiping off the table? No more. It will be a time to pray, a time to show special love.

6

You've Gained Eight Pounds Since Last Year

The doctor looked at my chart for a long time. I had come for my annual physical. He had completed my exam. His long, thin face surveyed the record as though I had just put dirt in his mouth.

He finally looked up. With an almost malicious grin, he said, "You've gained eight pounds since last year, Linda. I guess you already know that. If you continue to gain eight pounds a year, you'll weigh two hundred pounds in less than ten years. You really don't have the frame to carry two hundred pounds. What has happened to make you gain this extra weight?"

"Nothing," I replied trying to appear nonchalant. "It will come off easily. All I have to do is go back to my exercise program."

"It isn't the lack of exercise which causes you to gain weight."

"It isn't," I said naively. "Then what is it?"

"Overeating."

I spent the next fifteen minutes explaining to him in detail that he, of course, was wrong. I didn't eat too much. My eating habits haven't changed in the last several years.

"That could be true," he concluded, "but you are reaching middle age, you know."

"Middle age!" I gasped, scarcely able to catch my breath. "My mother isn't even middle-aged yet. I'm only thirty-two."

"True but your hormones could be changing. In order to compensate for a slowdown in your system, reduce your eating. Cut out all your between-meal snacks." He repositioned my chart to give emphasis, then slowly said, "Lose that eight pounds."

I slinked from the doctor's office. When I had come in, I was a young woman in the prime of life. Now I was a middle-aged matron, eight pounds overweight.

On the way home, I braced my ego back into an upright position. "I don't care what he thinks," I said out loud to myself. "I can't do anything about my weight. I don't overeat. I may be thirty-two but I most certainly don't eat too much."

I resolved that to prove my point I would write down every bite and morsel I put in my mouth between meals. I would make a survey of each mouthful, each crumb.

I started my written list the next morning. The first item was:

1) a teaspoon of sugar with a cup of tea.

That was quickly followed by:

2) a teaspoon of sugar for another cup of tea,
3) one cookie,
4) two pieces of fudge and a cookie crumb,
5) a bag of potato chips,
6) a cookie left from the crumb in item 4.

In a few minutes I realized that if I continued with my list through the morning, I would end up with writer's cramp and would never finish my housework.

To console myself I went to the kitchen for another cup of tea and a teaspoon of sugar. Walking out I picked up an apple and a piece of cake to tide me over until lunch.

"I guess I've got to chart another course," I said to myself when I ran out of paper for my food list. The writing system didn't seem to be helping me to lose the eight pounds. "Maybe a vigorous exercise plan will do the trick."

Now I've gone back to bike riding, swimming and walking. The eight pounds have steadfastly refused to melt away.

I am about to realize that the doctor could be right. I have to cut out my between-meal snacks. Even though Ephesians says that we are to submit one to another I find submission doesn't come easy for me.

It took me several years to even read the Scriptures which told me to submit to my husband. I just conveniently skidded over them. Now that the Lord has finally gotten through to me about the authority my husband has over me, I am starting to take more seriously the other verses about submission. It seems that each step in this walk is done with toes and heels dragging. I don't want any other authority in my life.

I'm not unlike most housewives who have been married for several years. I've learned to adjust to my husband's particular demands. Frank couldn't survive in a squeaky clean environment. He does want his meals attractive and on time, however. Adjusting my schedule to fit him has become pretty easy. That means that during most of the day, I can call the action about what I do, where I go, what I eat.

Sometimes it's good to have someone else put a stern finger of correction on a problem area. That's when the apostle Paul's admonition to submit ourselves one to another comes into the picture.

Then a really submissive spirit can start her shine. Instead of excuses and reasoning, compliance rules.

Yep, between-meal snacks have to go and so do those eight pounds.

7

Will the Real Mrs. Webb Please Stand Up

On March the first of this year, I got a request from my book publisher for a recent picture for their marketing files. Since housewives get few requests for their pictures, I didn't have one old, recent or decent. I went to a professional photographer and had one made.

I must make it clear in justice to him, he really seemed to know what he was doing. He straightened my shoulders and collar. He told me to look foxy, then took ten poses of my profile.

I was grateful that he didn't take any of the shots as straight-on poses since I inherited my father's Roman nose. (That's a nose which is roamin' all over your face.) When he sat me down for a side shot, I knew the Lord had indeed led me to this photographer.

The pictures came back in several days. I was pleased and rushed a copy to the marketing department.

I also sent one to a magazine who had published an article I had ghost written about a ninety-three-year-old woman, Mrs.

Marvis Webb, who lives in a retirement home.

Sending the portrait to the feature editor of the magazine, I told him that this was a recent photograph for their files. I included a handwritten note thanking him for sending the magazine containing my article on the retirement home. I told him the magazine had done a beautiful job with the layout for Mrs. Webb's piece.

About a week later, I got a polite letter from this editor. It read:

> Dear Mrs. Howard:
> Thank you for sending the picture of Mrs. Webb. We are putting it in our files. We at the magazine felt that her article about life in a retirement home was much needed and timely. We are hoping she will submit more articles sometime in the future.
> Sincerely yours,

When I read this letter, I didn't know whether to laugh or cry. I jerked a copy of the picture I had sent to them from my files and rushed into the family room where my daughter was having her piano lesson. "Nancy," I demanded poking the picture into the face of her piano teacher, "does this look like a ninety-three-year-old woman?"

"No," Nancy blinked obligingly. "But who am I to say? It isn't, is it? It looks a lot like you."

Actually I'm not sure what I should do now. I could have the picture retaken. This time I'd use heavy makeup and have my face lifted. Or I could ignore the whole thing. After all, it doesn't matter who other people think I am. In God's sight, I'm a person of worth.

Next time that magazine asks me for a picture though, I'm

going to send them a brief note saying, "Look in Mrs. Marvis Webb's file. The ninety-three-year-old woman in the picture is me."

8

The Subtotal Woman

Several years ago I rushed out and bought my copy of the *Total Woman*. I read with sheer delight Marabel Morgan's book which is a prescription for a happy marriage. I underlined interesting tidbits, took notes and determined that I too would become a Total Woman.

After at least two years of desperately trying to put her principles into practice, I've given up. I'm sorry, Marabel, I've tried. I'm destined to be subtotal forever.

My first failure came with the Saran Wrap caper. No woman in America needs to have that explained. A sure way, according to Marabel, to win your husband's undying love and devotion is to wrap yourself in Saran Wrap. Then you call him into the bedroom. What Marabel doesn't explain is how do you keep that stuff from sticking together. By the time you get the Saran Wrap out of the box and unraveled, you have a bedroom of tangled, shiny plastic and you are a sweaty mess.

You can never single-handedly wrap it around yourself.

You can bend, turn, coax and cry. Yet you aren't going to make it.

The romantic candlelit dinner suggested in the book was my next failure. My husband walked in, looked at the table and said, "That's beautiful. Let's turn on the lights."

"Okay," I thought, in harmony with the book. If he would be more comfortable with the lights on, we'll eat this way. We ate our salad immersed in the splendor of two candles and the overhead light.

Everything went well until one of the candles fell from its candlestick. The tablecloth caught on fire. Frank had to put it out with his coffee.

We resumed our dinner holding hands and giggling until there came a crashing thud through the doorway. The children had seen the flames and came to check on us. Somehow, the romantic spirit of the evening was broken.

The final blow in total womanhood came later on, however. It was when I tried to put the chapter entitled, "Costume Party," into practice. Marabel tells all aspiring total women that another way to their husbands' hearts is to adorn themselves with different costumes each night.

I figured that I could easily and inexpensively achieve this by visiting all the neighborhood garage sales. I was sure to come up with some bizarre goodies which no one else wanted. I was right.

Only the bizarre goodies I found didn't meet with the promised response from my husband.

I found this perfectly lovely pair of lounging pajamas made from a discarded shower curtain. It was a steal for only $1.50. Frank took one look and melted into fits of hysterical laughter. I was furious, naturally. That was not the way

Marabel had promised he would react.

One of the things she mentions over and over is boots. I got the impression that wearing boots was supposed to make your husband roar like a lion.

I found a nice pair for only $.30 at a garage sale across the street. Again, Frank remained unimpressed when I sauntered out wearing my nightie and boots.

Later that night, Frank did ask, "What ever made you think men's hiking boots were romantic?" Now could I help it if Marabel had left out one small but important detail. Men's hiking boots aren't sexy.

I'm certain that in the hands of the right person, the "Total Woman" concept could work wonders in a marriage. But I've put my book on the shelf for good.

I don't mind too much though. Frank loves me. His love keeps me total when I would otherwise be the subtotal woman.

9

Saturdays

Saturday is the day I blow my submission.

I'm a confirmed night person. I don't begin to function or even think until 11:30 A.M. Jerome Hines, the great opera star, once said that he couldn't even spit until noon. That's me.

Most mornings it works out fine. I get up. Stumble to the kitchen. I have my breakfast routine worked out so that I don't have to even open my eyes while preparing breakfast and packing Frank's lunch. The children all have their set patterns which are carefully planned and ordered.

After breakfast, Frank kisses me good-bye. We smile and he says, "God bless you and give you a good day."

I then say, "Same to you." He leaves for work.

Saturday, however, is different. My routine is broken. Unfortunately, the peace and security of our home is too.

By nine o'clock, I think to myself, "I'm going to have the family around all day. I might as well tell them what I think about the world situation." My tirade begins by explaining to Frank why I will no longer tolerate his brown eyes or the hair on his chest.

From there I digress into the more trivial things about him which bother me. Frank patiently and lovingly takes it as long as he can. Finally when he can no longer bear the verbal beatings, he gets up and leaves the room.

"How dare you leave when I'm trying to talk to you!" I cry. "That's what's wrong with our marriage. No communication!"

About noon, I begin to wake up. I remember the nightmare of a terrible argument. Then I realize it was no nightmare, only another typical Saturday. Even though it's the day I invariably blow all my submission, Frank and the children still love me.

That could be one of the greatest compensations about being a housewife. My boss loves me and I love him. We are a family.

After high school, I attended a secretarial college. Over and over again we were warned by our professors that single women shouldn't get romantically involved with their bosses even if both parties are unattached.

When Frank and I were married, I became a full-time housewife and he became my boss. For us romantic involvement is one of the bonuses of our relationship.

Sure we tend to show each other our cruder, most ugly sides occasionally; but we have love. The Bible teaches that love covers a multitude of sins. I'm grateful for that love covering every time I blow my submission and especially on Saturday.

10

Submission
or New Plants

In our home, we live by the scriptural concept that the husband is the head of the house. Recently this rule met with the supreme test. Frank put his foot down right into a newly potted fern and said, "Linda, there will be no more plants brought into this house. I can't even walk without stepping into an aloe or a pineapple."

I couldn't blame him, of course. It seems I have become addicted to the smell of fresh potting soil and liquid fertilizer.

Like most plant people, I had started slowly. At first I purchased a small hanging basket at my local nursery. With proper care and nutrients, it soon blossomed into a luscious variegated wall of green. I was hooked.

My birthdays and Christmas brought more growing things. Soon I found myself enjoying the wonder of plants growing in the house. There was no weeding or work required after these lovelies were planted. The only physical work was carrying a glass of water to them for their weekly drink.

Soon the family room was adorned with thirty-five hanging

baskets and fifteen potted plants carefully placed on the television, chests and floor.

I rearranged the kitchen window and put shelves in it to accommodate even more plants. When we changed our guest room into my office, I decorated it in early philodendron and Danish macrame.

Frank did not even complain when I began my campaign on the bathroom. My motto became, "A happy bath is a green bath." I sensed a distinct change in his attitude toward my little green dears, however, when I put a hanging Spanish moss in front of the rack where the wash cloth had once hung. "Where am I supposed to put my rag now?" Frank calmly asked.

"Don't worry about it," I quietly reassured him. "You're so clever. I'm sure you'll think of something.

"You'll love that new Spanish moss though. My biweekly plant guide says that the shower is the best place to hang potted plants. They thrive and flourish from the steam and moisture coming from our baths."

Perhaps his breaking point came when I began to cut out diagrams and plans for skylights in each room which required massive reconstruction of the roof.

Or maybe it came the day my parents brought a trunk full of new ferns and moss just right for our bedroom.

No matter. I have decided that Frank is right. I must stop adding new plants to my indoor garden, and I intend to tell him so. That is, just as soon as I can find him through my forest of green.

11

I'm Never Late Unless . . .

Grace was accompanying me on a speaking engagement to a nearby town. Arriving at her apartment right on time, I blew the car horn and waited. My friend finally came out breathless.

Huffing and puffing, she stared at me with disbelief. Then she muttered almost under her breath, "You're on time!"

I ignored the slight slur in her voice while she applied her makeup, combed her hair and put on her shoes. "I never expected you to be on time," she said now, clearly irritated.

Most of my friends would never believe me, but I'm never late unless I go somewhere with my husband. Like me, Frank is a proverbial early bird, unless we're together.

For years I was not sure why we seemed to hold each other back from our appointed tasks. After the episode with Grace, I decided to examine the situation to try and make it better. After careful study, I'm afraid there is no cure.

First of all, we get in each other's way. Frank is invariably in the bathroom when I need to brush my teeth. I can plan to brush my teeth at the beginning of my preparation or at the end. It doesn't matter. He is always there shaving. That wouldn't be too bad except our otherwise adequate bathroom is squeakingly small in one place. Right in front of the sink.

In order for both of us to stand in front of the sink at the same time, we have to stand sideways. Brushing my teeth with cold water while Frank is shaving in hot water is bad enough but standing sideways makes both operations lengthy and painful.

Second, there is no one available to answer the children's questions. We can go for three weeks without any one of them even grunting at us. But once that bedroom door closes in preparation for some appointment, they stand in line with questions. There is a continual, "Mother! Daddy!" echoing in plaintive tones from the hall.

Naturally one question always leads to another.

"Can I have a candy bar?"

"Yes."

"Can I have all the candy bars?"

"No."

"Why?"

"They will ruin your dinner."

"When are we going to have dinner?"

The dialogue is endless. Such conversation usually develops into a discourse on world hunger.

I stand in my slip and pantyhose with my mouth and nose sticking through the crack in the door answering questions about everything. The moon. Sex. Prayer. Traffic. Jet propulsion. Freckles. Why there'll be no more Saturn 5 launches. The list of topics is without end.

Finally we get ready to walk out the door only fifteen

minutes late. There is one more agonizing delay. I can't find my shoes and there is no one, absolutely no one, to help me. Frank, of course, is no help. He is much too busy trying to find his keys.

Our ride to the place where we're to be is fraught with just as many interferences. The car always needs gas. The drive to the service station is an act of faith as we pray that the last of the fumes will get us to the nearest gas pump.

I'm sure it isn't true but it seems that the city discovers our route ahead of time in order to destroy and tear up at least one street on which we're to travel. We're detoured, bumped, jostled, jerked and most painfully slowed down.

When at last we arrive tired and bruised, some unsympathetic soul will say, "Oh, it's the Howards. Why, you're only an hour late. How did you ever manage to make it here so early?"

Can we ever learn to take these kinds of little annoyances and scoldings and turn them into our good? It's hard enough to be criticized when you're wrong yet unjust criticism is even harder to stomach. But, if Romans 8:28, "All things work together for good to them that love God, to them who are the called according to his purpose," is true then they can.

Perhaps this is one of the areas that we'll have to become like Paul. He wrote from prison, "I have learned that in whatever condition I find myself, I am content."

To be misunderstood is hard to bear no matter what the circumstance but not impossible. Several years ago I saw my parents come under a terrible attack of unjustified criticism. I blistered and wanted to set the record straight then and there. My parents, however, smiled and told me patiently to stop worrying about it.

Finally, I turned in frustration to mother and said, "How

can you stand there and let that woman say those things about you?"

Mother smiled at daddy and said, "Honey, when you've been through as many hurts as we have, you learn it's not worth the effort. The Lord will take care of it much better than we can."

Even though I don't want to have to go through hard times, I want that kind of peace and assurance to reign in my life. With the Lord's help and comfort I can learn not to bristle under the stern eye of a friend who gently scolds, "Why must you always be late?"

12

The "Best Looker" in the House

There is a comic strip called the "Jackson Twins." They are very pretty twins who have a little brother. One day the mother of the twins overheard a conversation her son was having with a friend. "Mom," he explained to the boy, "is the best looker in the house."

The mother pranced into the room proud as peaches. "Thank you, son," she said looking in the mirror. "Do you really think I'm the best looker in the house?"

"Oh, yes," he said. Then the son added, "You can find anything. You are definitely the best looker in the whole house. Whenever anything is lost you can always find it."

I wonder if all women are born "good lookers" or if it is an occupational trait developed from much practice.

It is interesting to see how my children are developing their finding and looking talents.

Mark, our son, has a special technique he uses to look for almost everything. He stands in the middle of the room and turns around three times. "I can't find it," he says finally. "I have looked over the whole room three times. It just isn't here. I can't find it anywhere."

Carol, who is only four years old, uses a similar technique. Only she stands in the middle of the room and bursts into tears. That way someone else is bound to take pity on her and find the missing article.

Leah, however, is my best looker. If I can ever get her down to looking, she can locate anything in the house. She will overturn, uproot, use Marine search out and destroy tactics in order to find her prey.

The other day Frank needed a special pencil to complete a drawing he was working on. First he sent Mark for it. "Go into the bedroom and find my blue pencil with purple stripes," his father instructed him. Mark went into the room. He turned around three times and came back with his "I looked everywhere" story.

Carol was the next one sent. She came back in about thirty seconds in pathetic tears. "It's not in there, daddy. I can't find it."

Then Leah was sent to find the elusive pencil. In only fifty seconds flat she came, breathless but victorious, bearing the pencil. "Where did you find it?" I asked.

"Oh, it wasn't in the bedroom. It was at Stacy's. You know the house on the corner. I found it over there. Carol or somebody had left it yesterday. It was a simple matter of going and getting it."

Leah settled down to watch television. Frank scratched his head with his retrieved pencil and mumbled to me, "I wonder how she knew it was at Stacy's house."

"I can't tell," I said in great admiration for my older daughter. "All I know is she sure is the 'best looker' in the house."

The "Best Looker" in the House

Jesus told two stories which are recorded in the Gospel of Luke that relate to looking for lost objects. There was a man who had one hundred sheep and one of them got lost. When he realized that it was missing, he went out on the mountains and searched until he found his sheep.

The second story was about a woman who had ten coins. She lost one. In order to find her lost treasure she cleaned and scoured, sweeping her house clean and finding her coin.

Bible scholars tell us that this coin was important to her because these ten coins were worn on a band around her forehead to signify that she was a virgin.

As every housewife knows, that wasn't the case at all. It was the day before payday and those coins were her children's lunch money. She didn't have any bread in the house to make sandwiches and no other money.

That is the only crisis which could produce such a frantic search.

In addition to the obvious point of these two stories that God loves us enough to make unbelievable sacrifices, there is also a subtle undercurrent of teaching which can be found in these parables.

In these two stories Jesus shows us a basic difference between men and women.

What did the man find? A sheep, a large object, a very large object. Where did he go? To the mountain. A big open area. He probably stumbled over that sheep before he found it.

The woman, however, lost a small object. A coin. How did she find it? She looked in every corner and crevice of her home. She left no old newspaper unturned.

Here, Jesus is teaching us that the attitudes of men and women in many areas of life are different. Women are basically good lookers. They go into minute detail. They observe every inch of space.

Men seem to be able to grasp an oversight of situations. While I'm dissecting a problem into ten thousand pieces, Frank is able to come up with a logical oversight. More times than not, his oversight is the key to getting the tiny grit picked up.

My approach to the Scriptures is different from my husband's also. I delight in picking apart every verse and going into divergent oscillation over the tense of a verb. Frank teaches and studies from whole chapters at a time.

Both pictures are necessary. We need the male oversight. We need the female lookers.

In practical as well as spiritual matters, we have started to appreciate the other's natural talents to be able to see different things in each situation. I'm learning to appreciate Frank's oversight and he's beginning to take advantage of "my good looks."

13

Extracurricular Duties

Over and over I'm asked how I find time to write, keep a house and tend to three children, one a preschooler. I always smile and mumble something about organization.

I think the time has come to let the whole truth be known. Yes, the time I need for writing has come from organization. Yet I learned this organization from my extracurricular household duties.

Extracurricular household duties are those things you normally do which wouldn't be put into a job description sheet. Like the afternoon you went out to pull up a few weeds from the front yard and ended up single-handedly spading and uprooting the entire front lawn with only a shovel and pick. Or perhaps making a leisure suit for your husband. Or finishing one of those Erica Wilson crewel embroidery masterpieces with only twenty-five million stitches.

In the past year since I have begun to write on a regular basis, I have let most of my extracurricular activities slide. I have found that I have hours and hours to devote to writing.

Now I don't mean that I have laid them aside forever. I fully intend to finish crocheting the twenty-four skeins of yarn I have which will make an afghan for each member of the family. I also plan to make many more dresses, suits and daisy coverlets. For the time being though, I have put them aside for other things.

Yet with setting them aside, I have come to realize how much time they take.

I can write a three-page magazine article in the same time it takes to coax embroidery thread through the eye of a needle. I can edit and have that same article in the mail in the time it takes to flip through one Vogue pattern book.

I can finish the rough draft of a complete book in the same time it takes to finish one lounging suit.

The most frustrating thing for me is not that these extra things we housewives do take so much time, but how little they are appreciated.

A person will "Ooh" and "Aah" over a one-page 409-word article published in our church paper. But when I show them my macrame wall hanging, they simply look away with detachment and an uninterested smile.

Do they care that it took me six weeks just to learn how to tie a square knot? No. Do they care that I have sacrificed hours and three fingernails to that project which they casually turn away from? No.

One day when we wives and mothers receive our reward, I think we will be amazed. The Lord will turn and smile. He will not have overlooked the days and weeks spent on one crocheted bedroom slipper. He will know how many times you had to pull out that one seam to make it lay just right so your daughter wouldn't be embarrassed because the collar on her dress kept flying into her mouth.

He may be the only one who knows and appreciates the hours spent washing the tar from your son's bathing suit. Then I guess He is the only who really matters after all.

Yes, when the whole truth is known, we'll see all the time we have spent on these extracurricular household chores. I only hope the Lord has someone there to catch us. For when we see how much time they take each day, we will probably faint from exhaustion.

14

They Never Notice

"My family never seems to notice all the little things I do for them," my friend Shirley complained one day. "There is only one time they notice at all. That's if I don't do them."

I had to sympathize with her. Even though I know Frank is unusual because he pays attention to many of the things I do, he does sometimes slip.

I can spend twenty minutes everyday washing breakfast dishes. Not one soul mentions it. If I don't do them, that's a different tale. Some devious magnetism draws him into the kitchen the minute he comes home from work. With a shy grin, he asks, "Aren't these the breakfast dishes?"

I can bleach, scrub and 409 the children's socks until they're squeaky clean. When do they notice? The week I throw them into the laundry tub without all my additives. Then they say, "Mom, why can't you get my socks clean like Aunt Dola Jean and Aunt Ferne do?"

I can spend one half of my day turning out lights and adjusting the drapes to keep maximum sunlight in the house.

When do they notice? The one day in three years I leave the bathroom light burning. Then Carol will walk up to me and say, "Mommy, you left the light on. You know daddy wants us to cut it off."

There is a television commercial which shows a woman who is wondering how she can get her family to notice all the little extra things she does for them. She puts Downy in the laundry. She cuts their toe nails and clips their hair but no one seems to care.

Well, I don't have to worry about that at all. You see God has said, "I'll use the foolish things to confound the wise." I've learned to take advantage of what my friend complained about. I know exactly how to get my family to notice the things I do. I just don't do them for a short period. They notice every time.

15

The Third Basic Fear

Psychologists say we are born with only two basic fears. There is the fear of falling and the fear of loud and sudden noises. I contend that there is a third basic fear which is inborn. It is the fear that we will never be heard. That's why children are natural born naggers.

Now a sensitive adult, especially a wife and mother, is never a nag. She is a reminder. There is a definite difference between a reminder and a nag. A nag speaks in a whining monotone. A reminder usually yells. I'm a very good reminder.

My children did not escape this third basic fear. They have been nags since the day they were born. By now they are bonafide, professional naggers.

It should be explained here that there are two distinct types of nagging. One is the normal verbal nagging. The other is what I call physical nagging. A physical nagger is a person who begins to lightly tap you while he or she talks. I have three permanent bruise spots. One is on the arm where Mark hits me to get attention. One is my elbow where Leah hits me and one is on my hip where Carol hits me. Physical nagging always starts out as a light tap but the blows build in intensity by the second. If I don't answer by fourteen seconds, the arm, elbow or hip would become permanently disabled from the pain.

In order to demonstrate how a person's day will go who lives with three nags, let me tell you what happened today.

I was having a nice telephone conversation with a friend. Mark came charging in breathless. "Mother, I've been trying to get you on the phone for half an hour. Mother! Are you still on the phone? Mother?"

After fifteen repeated mothers, I said, "What is it, Mark? Can't you see I'm on the phone?"

"May I go to the beach?"

"Son, you got up at six this morning to go to the beach. You've been at the beach three times already and it's only 9:30 A.M."

"Well, you told me to come home every hour to check in. Can I go back now?"

"I don't know."

"When will you know?"

"Mark, leave me alone for a minute."

"Then I can go to the beach?"

"Mark!" Mark then positioned himself at my bedroom door and I returned to my conversation. Leah came in.

"Mother, all the girls have come over and want me to go to the clubhouse. Can I go? Mother! Can I go?"

"What, Leah?"

"Can I go?"

"Go where?"

"To the clubhouse."

"Leah, wait a minute. Let me finish my conversation." Leah dramatically and with great melodrama threw herself across the bed. Carol came into the room.

"Can I go to Stacy's?" Carol asked lightly tapping me on the hip. I know that she can't be ignored because she has started the physical nagging. Ignoring physical nagging means death within sixty seconds.

"Carol, I'll be off in one minute. Ask me later."

When I hung up the telephone receiver, I looked at them. "Now, what did you want?"

"The beach," Mark reminded me.

"You can go to the beach. Be back—"

"In an hour," Mark finished the sentence as he left.

"Can I go to the clubhouse?" Leah asked.

"Be back—"

"In an hour," Leah finished my sentence as she rushed out the door.

"Can I go to Stacy's?"

"Yes, Carol, be back—"

"In an hour," Carol finished the sentence as she left. Carol reappeared in about fifteen seconds. "Mommy, what's an hour?"

Can someone ever overcome the third basic fear? The answer is definitely, "Yes." It's overcome each time I listen.

In spite of my schedule, dirty diapers, and the continual chatter which forges into my life, nagging is conquered when I put enough importance on the words my family shoots my way to listen, really listen.

16

Don't Judge Me
by My Children's Pajamas

In Proverbs 31 God is describing His perfect woman. I always skip over verse twenty-one quickly. It says, "She is not afraid of the snow for her household: for all her household are clothed in scarlet."

In teaching this verse several years ago, some advice my mother had given to me came back. "Linda," she said, "your relationship with the Lord is usually judged by the world and other Christians from the appearance of your children and the clothes they wear."

We live in Florida. I am not at all afraid of the snow but I would hate for my spirituality to be judged by the pajamas my children wear to bed.

Mark has always been the nonconformist of the family. He has refused since the age of two years and three months to wear pajamas at all. He sleeps in a pair of baggies. Incidentally, it's the same pair of baggies he has worn for three years.

Leah inherited a caftan from a girl friend. It's completely

worn out and is held together by one thread at the shoulders. For the past year that has been her nightly uniform. I have hidden it. Thrown it away. I even took it across the river and chunked it into a burning incinerator. Each night it miraculously reappears. It is three sizes too large and drags to the ground collecting dirt, germs and mildew.

Carol would have to take the prize though. About six months ago, I went through all my old nightgowns and pulled out the most ragged ones I could find for the girls to use as dress-up clothes. Carol has adopted four of them for her nightly apparel. Leah's caftan is three sizes too large, Carol's garb is thirty sizes too large.

Her favorite gown is pale, washed-out blue. The shoulder straps hang below her belly button. The rest of the gown trails ungracefully under foot and behind her. It has a large split right in the front. She uses the hole as a pocket. She prances delicately to bed with her head held high tripping over the yards of excess material. If she ever has to get up in the middle of the night to go to the bathroom, she will undoubtedly end up sprawled on the floor.

I wonder, if the angel of the Lord came one night to judge me by Proverbs 31, would I fail? Maybe not. These are garments of love for the children. Just like my husband's old painting pants, which have many colors of paint smeared and wiped on them and my lifelong companions, a pair of jeans. They are older than the children and the only "pre-baby" garment I have that I can wiggle into. Even though they are not fit for outside eyes I love to wear them on occasion just because I like the way they feel.

I know that we are warned over and over in the Scriptures to not love the things of the world and that admonition must be kept if we are to continue to maintain a heavenly minded attitude. But even Paul asked for his manuscripts, books and a special coat while he was in jail.

Garments of love are important for children, husbands and housewives who can continue to worm their way into old, loved clothes. Paul would understand this and I believe the angel of the Lord would too.

17

The Who-Did-It Game

In our house we have a game we play. It's called Who Did It. The game is played at all times during the day. It could be started by any member of the family. The rules are simple. Someone says, "Who did this?"

Then each remaining member of the family echoes in chorus, "I didn't do it."

Usually Frank or I take the "Who did it" part. Mark, Leah and Carol sing the "I didn't do it" back to us.

I don't care what the problem is. It doesn't even matter how much incriminating evidence points to the guilty party. I can watch one of the children drop an orange peel on the floor and ask, "Who did this?"

The immediate answer without a second of hesitation is, "I didn't."

Several years ago I decided to adopt a different variation. I would say to one of them, "Why did you do this?"

Unfortunately I found the answer didn't change. It remained the same, "I didn't do it. Really I didn't."

It is interesting to see how each child plays the game. Mark is the kind of person who is never moved by circumstance. Last month when there was a prophecy that an enormous tidal wave would hit and completely wipe out Florida, he only smiled and said, "Oh, good. I'm glad I got my new surfboard. Do you think it will hit near here so I could ride the big one?"

That's the way he plays the game. Unmoved and unconcerned. The other night Frank and I walked into the house. We had taken a bike ride together. We had been gone about an hour and Mark had been left in charge. When we got back, the door had been left open, and a herd of flies had overtaken the lit up portion of the house. The piano had coke spilled on the keys. The television had been smeared with fingerprints. It seemed like every dish and bowl in the house had been taken from the cabinets and put in the middle of the family room floor.

"Who did this?" I demanded.

Mark raised weakly from his position leaning against one elbow. Surveying the damage, he mumbled, "I didn't."

Leah is totally different. She is a sensitive, emotional child. She's probably the world's greatest prima donna. She immediately threw herself onto the couch and burst into a torrent of seemingly uncontrolled tears. "I didn't do it," she wailed.

Carol, our four-year-old, is happy-go-lucky and tender. However, she remains unaffected by almost everything. She plays the game different from all the rest. She looked up from her play, smiled and said, "I didn't do it." Then she pointed to her brother and sister still grinning, "Mark and Leah did it."

I suspect that all families play this game but I'm beginning to get tired of it. Recently when I ask, "Who did this?" I don't give anyone a chance to answer. I throw up my hands and say, "Oh, I know. None of you did it. I confess then. I'm the culprit. I did it."

Even though it's said in sarcastic humor, in a real way, that's what Jesus did for us. He took the blame for all the mess and disruptions we've caused in the past and will cause in the future.

It could be that it's the only way to reach hearts. Yesterday after I confessed to the crime, Leah turned and said, "Oh, no, mother. I did it."

18

So Spiritually Minded You're No Earthly Good

I had often heard the old cliché, "He's so spiritually minded he's no earthly good." I never knew exactly what it meant until about two years ago.

I was in the grocery store and saw a friend. I had met Mary Lou at the Little League baseball games. We had shared splinters, bruises, home runs, the thrill of victory and the agony of defeat for almost a whole year. But I had not known she was a Christian.

There in the grocery store while waiting in the check-out line, we began to talk about the Lord. Her older daughter attended our church and Mary Lou was inquiring to be sure that she could continue to get the church newspaper while she was at college. We cheerfully talked about the deep things of the Lord and the joy of Jesus.

I pushed my cart into the correct position and started to unload my groceries. All along, we were happily discussing spiritual matters.

At this particular store, the unloading procedure goes

something like this: You take out your groceries on the left side of the check-out counter. Your cart stays on the left side. You move with your groceries to the right side where the cashier adds them up. You pay and leave. Only if you have a heavy load which requires you to use a cart to take out your groceries, do you ever see your cart again. You are separated from your cart by the cashier and the cash register.

Usually that's a fine arrangement. That is unless you've been enthralled in a spiritual conversation and forgotten you brought your well-behaved two-year-old and left her in the cart.

That's exactly what I did. I left my cart and my daughter. I brisked out the store and headed for home.

It wasn't until I was cruising into my driveway that I realized the back seat was very quiet.

"Carol," I called casually.

No answer.

I stopped the car and searched the back seat. "Carol!" I yelled. "She must be here," I said out loud to myself. "I didn't leave her at the grocery store, I'm sure."

No Carol. Whipping the car around, running over a trash can and three prized pieces of shrubbery, I headed back to the store.

Waiting outside was my friend, Mary Lou. "I knew you would be back," she said. "One of your neighbors was in the store too. She volunteered to take Carol home for you."

I turned to rush back home, "Was she crying?" I asked Mary Lou as I made my exit.

"No, she didn't cry at all."

When I got back home, Carol was in the arms of the neighbor. They were taking a walk. Carol came to me lovingly. She stared into my eyes and patted my face. The only thing she said to me was, "You left me. You left me. You left me."

Since then no one has to explain to me what being so spiritually minded you're no earthly good means. All I have to do is ask Carol. She'll tell me. It means leaving your baby at the grocery store because you've become involved in talking about the Lord and forgotten her.

19

Fasting
and the Housewife

As beneficial as fasting is to the Christian, there is a tremendous disadvantage which is only known to the ordinary housewife.

I will not even have to go into detail for a haggard, hungry woman who has gone into the grocery store to pick up a simple loaf of bread while observing a day of fasting.

Invariably you exit with $29.17 worth of junk foods and assorted candies.

This hazard will never be found on any Jamie Buckingham tape or in a Derek Prince book on fasting. It is an occupational handicap known only to the housewife.

Today I was fasting. I turned down the apple and cinnamon coffee cake for breakfast. It was not even hard to refuse a luncheon invitation. I brought my preschooler home and fed her a cup of soup and contented myself with extra work.

Then came that fatal trip to the corner grocery store for a loaf of bread. The first thing I spied was a huge mound of candy. It touched the ceiling and took up thirty-four square feet of floor space. It was positioned in the middle of the front door.

Normally, I breeze by such temptations without a second glance. Today, in my hunger, I paused to smell. The peanuts covered with chocolate mingled with the malted milk balls and created an orchestration of dancing taste buds. My mouth watered, drooled and dripped.

Bracing myself for the rest of the trip, I picked up a six pack of candy bars and quickly headed for the bread counter. Soft drinks, marshmallows all breezed into my basket unbeckoned. Finally, I realized that I must stop this madness. This was junk food. God is concerned about our bodies.

Eggs were on sale. I purchased two dozen and headed again for the bread counter. Lunch meat, cereal, dog food, flour all made their way into my cart. I turned my direction back to the bread counter.

At last, after passing the cream puffs, orange juice and fruit, I got my bread and swiftly headed to the check-out counter.

There is no way I can explain the amount of the check-out tape. I slowly walked out of the store shaking my head. My mind swirled with assorted salted nuts, Fruit Loops and bagels.

I spent the next hour unloading my groceries and praying. I have come to this conclusion.

I shall plan my fast days differently. Never again on my days of abstinence shall I enter the "no man's land" of the faster, the grocery store.

20

Whole-Wheat Bread

Before I take on any new fads or good ideas from other people, I always ask, "Is there any chance I could develop this into a phobia that will require deliverance?"

If the answer is yes, I usually say, "Just forget it."

When I had to be delivered from whole-wheat bread, I knew that there was a problem area in my life which makes me prone to extremes.

Actually whole-wheat bread was only the beginning. I started using only whole wheat soon after I got pregnant with our third child. Before a month was gone, I was not only making my own bread but grinding the wheat, churning the butter, and squeezing olives for the oil.

Our menus included such delicacies as homemade yogurt soup, lentil pie and whole-wheat everything.

I bought fertilized eggs, cottage cheese cultures, raw sugar, and uncolored Kool-Aid. We bought honey by the six gallon container and sea water salt by the case. I led the peanut butter campaign in our town for truth in peanut butter advertising.

I called or wrote all food processers who carried brand names in our local grocery store asking for sworn statements that their ingredient lists were not falsified.

One night Frank, my husband, looked stoically into my eyes. "Linda," he said with measured calmness, "I think this obsession you have for natural foods has gotten out of hand."

It was true and I knew it.

The struggle out of my health food hang-up has been a battle supreme. I have to tear myself away from labels to be sure that I won't read and analyze them. One television special on food additives can throw me into a week of renewed letter writing and campaigns.

Yesterday, however, I won a great victory in my battle. I went into the store and came out with a whole case of Coca-Cola.

21

Pride Comes Before the Fall

Today I did everything right, except one.

I cleaned the house well. I cooked a good meal of hot, homemade chili with just the right seasonings. I wrote five or six pages of rough draft material. I did everything right, except one.

I forgot we were having company for dinner.

I had set the table for four because our older daughter, Leah, was eating at church. I used the special china, matching glasses, bowls and napkins. I had a nice basket of crackers in the center of the table and tangy iced tea. Supper was ready right when Frank came in from work at six o'clock. Our hungry dinner guests arrived at 6:15.

I had just finished my first bowl of chili. The children were asking to be excused. Frank was asking, "What's for dessert?" There was no way I could bluff my way out of the situation when the company arrived. I simply had forgotten they were coming even though I invited them only yesterday.

Oh, I had spent most of the afternoon patting myself on the

back. "You're finally beginning to put it all together, old girl," I said as I surveyed the pleasant fruit of my handiwork. "It only takes a little bit of practice, a lot of patience and great organization. But you've got it. You've finally got all the pieces in place."

God has a tremendous sense of timing. For I had just finished congratulating myself on the job well done when the knock came at the door. We let four-year-old Carol answer it because it couldn't be for us. Then our company came in.

The Bible says, "Pride comes before the fall." Well, I know what that means. I've experienced the pride of a day well done. Most importantly, I've experienced the ego-splitting fall. There is no way you can feel pride when you forget the one little detail I forgot. Company for dinner.

22

Dinner Will Be Ready in a Minute

Frank says that the way I get compliments on my cooking is simple. I make our guests wait until they are one step from the door of starvation. Then I serve the meal. By that time, anything would taste good, including old shoe leather.

I remember one evening we invited a couple, Ralph and Wilemena, and their two children over for Saturday dinner. They were to come at five-thirty. At five o'clock I had to make an emergency trip to the grocery store for some goodies.

I zipped out leaving Mark and Leah at home. I was sure I would be back in time to meet our guests so I didn't tell the children to expect them. Frank had to work that day so he wasn't home when the couple arrived. They were about fifteen minutes early.

Our children didn't know the couple was coming for dinner and told them so. When our guests asked where I was, the children had a mental block and couldn't remember that either.

Ralph and Wilemena came into the house warily. By now

they suspected that they had gotten their dates mixed, but since they were hungry they decided to chance it and stick around. Wilemena went into the kitchen. She found no apparent preparations had been made toward supper.

They were ready to slip out quietly when I bombed in the door. I apologized for not being home when they arrived and went into the kitchen for a few last-minute preparations for dinner. All I had to do was fix the salad, meat, vegetables and dessert.

"Dinner will be ready in a few minutes," I called from the kitchen.

"Good," Ralph said, "I'm really hungry. I worked all day and I haven't had a bite since breakfast. I didn't even take time to stop for lunch. I could eat a mule."

Frank came in about that time. Wilemena came into the kitchen. We chatted while the men entertained themselves.

When we finally sat down to eat it was eight-thirty. Ralph had begun to chew on the tablecloth from hunger.

He ate his first course lustily. "My, my this is delicious," he slurped. "Best salad I ever ate."

"Thank you," I said, serving him mounds of meat and potatoes.

He ate with great abandonment. In a few minutes he threw me a pleading glance which asked for more. By now his wife, Wilemena, was beginning to become a bit aggravated.

"Ralph," she said. "Don't eat so much. Remember your diet."

"I can't help it," he said between mouthfuls. "It's just so delicious."

Wilemena apologized. I merely blushed sheepishly and replied with humility, "It's all right. It happens all the time."

After Ralph and Wilemena left, Frank stared at me with a

disapproving eye. "You had to do it again, didn't you?"

"What did I do? Cook a great meal?"

"No. You made them wait until they were starving before you served the food."

"Well," I said leaving the room, "it's a perfect way to get a few compliments."

23

The Five-Minute Miracle

Ruth Wainer, a housewife who works full-time as a secretary, was telling me the other day that in one and a half hours she and her boys had cleaned the house, the yard, and washed and waxed both cars. "Now, don't tell me that wasn't a miracle," she said in conclusion.

Even though I have never tried to do all those things together, I do know about the five-minute miracles the Lord performs for me occasionally.

The Lord usually reserves this kind of miracle for special days. Those are the days the washing machine water has backed up all the way to the bathroom. The dryer has rebelled and refused to dry another piece of clothing. The refrigerator has been completely overtaken by a mad scientist who specializes in bacterial growth and the children have the stomach virus.

It's on those days which seem choreographed by Erma Bombeck that the merciful, gracious Lord of the universe reaches down and heals my house in five minutes.

I have seen my family room in such a condition that only an earthquake could straighten it out. Yet the Lord will swoop down and touch it. He truly can bring order out of chaos. The living room may look as though the police benefit ball was held there last night and 250 people attended. But He can fix that in an instant.

I'm not sure how the Lord does it. I'm never quite sure when or where He will stoop down to perform this miracle, but I have seen Him do it too many times for me to ever be a doubter.

The other afternoon I was busy writing. I had become involved in some television scripts. On the days I get absorbed in my writing, I usually let my four-year-old have a pretty free reign in the family room. My office also becomes her study room where she cuts, colors and turns the floor and furniture into a bit of modern art. As usual the office was tossed with scraps of scissor cuttings and crayons. The family room was a shambles.

I had had two luncheon guests, both unexpected. One had come at eleven o'clock. The other showed up about twelve-thirty. Because I was pushing a deadline, I left our lunch dishes. The living room followed close behind the dining room. You could smell the bathroom within one hundred feet.

I had just settled down to my typing when there was a knock at the door.

Standing poised wreathed in smiles were relatives from out of state. They had dropped in for a three-day visit. At first, shock set in. I was thrilled to see them but the house—Then I remembered the Lord gracious and mighty was with me. As I invited them into the house, I prayed, "Help."

Can you ever explain the Lord? He did it again and

everything soon was in order. If our guests noticed the confusion, they didn't mention it.

I sat and entertained them until the children came home. As each one was welcomed, hugged and kissed, I straightened and picked up. Then as the children left to change their clothes, I loaded them down with books and junk to take to their rooms.

When Frank came in from work, he called me into the bedroom. "Are you all right?" he asked. "Everything looks clean and straight. I know you had a deadline to meet. Was everything clean when they came?"

"No," I said honestly, "but the Lord did it again. I think He sent a legion of angels who cleaned everything up."

Oh, yes, I know God is a miracle worker. I've seen Him perform too many five-minute miracles with my house to ever be a doubter.

24

Your Refrigerator Has Spots

I don't care how many television commercials there are which claim otherwise, I am not the only one who has spots on her refrigerator.

I don't mean these spots are the small unseen kind which look something like fingerprints. I mean large black spots that strongly resemble dirt. Actually I'm convinced these spots come as standard equipment for families who have children.

In order to confirm my suspicions, I have done a sort of mini-survey of refrigerators all over the southern part of the United States. My survey proved beyond reasonable doubt what I had always known. If there are any children in the home, the refrigerator in that place has come equipped with spots.

Even though you won't find this spotty addition on any sales brochure, they do come as standard equipment. They are painted on by some kind of special formula. The spots will wipe off just as though they aren't there. As soon as you turn your back though, they reappear.

Other kitchen appliances come similarly equipped. Freezers, hot water heaters, stoves, sinks. Many kitchen cabinets are also painted with this mysterious paint. Sometimes you will even find them on bathroom fixtures and cabinets.

There is a disturbing thing about those spots. If you don't have children, they aren't included on any of your appliances.

I have seen mature older women who should have known about this mysterious paint come into a home with children and ask with a sense of superior delight, "Did you know there are spots on your refrigerator?"

Many young mothers haven't been informed that the spots have been put there deliberately by the manufacturer. They will apologetically dig out the 409 and begin to scrub down the offender.

Not me. Oh, I confess in the past, I have been caught in that trap but no more. I scrubbed my refrigerator twenty-three times in one afternoon only to have the spots come back after each rubbing. That's the day I faced the stark reality that they are standard equipment.

Now when I'm faced with someone who discovers my spots, I smile casually. "Yes," I nonchalantly say. "They came with the refrigerator. They blend well with the walls and decor in the rest of the house.

"I think it's a special formula of paint called 'Dirty Fingers.' If you're interested, I'll be glad to give you the model number of our refrigerator. However, you may have to put in a special order to get one just like ours."

It's strange but with all the people who have noticed my spots, I don't know of even one of them who has ordered one for themselves.

25

I Don't Need
a Calculator

About a year ago, I inherited a calculator from my husband. He had just gotten a new improved model for himself and decided to give me his old one. To be perfectly honest, I didn't want it.

"No. Thank you," I politely turned it down. "I don't need a calculator."

Actually I have abhorred the way I've seen calculators take over perfectly good minds. I saw a woman in the grocery store only yesterday who had to take out her hand calculator in order to count her children. What made it even more disgusting was that she had only one child.

Men and women all over the United States and Japan who have before prided themselves as good adders are now totally dependent on a three by four inch mass of blinking lights in order to do the simplest additions.

Ask them to subtract without their calculators and they immediately have an attack of the digital fidgets.

Perhaps the reason I am so touchy about this subject is that adding has never been easy for me. In order to pass math my first five years in school, I had to depend on the law of averages and some blind, Spirit-guided guesses.

It wasn't until I was in business college and took a course in speed adding that I could add at all. Because they used several mental tricks, I was finally able to catch on. Now to expect me to turn over this knowledge to a few push buttons and light emitting diodes is just too much.

For a whole year, I kept my calculator in the desk drawer under paper clips, toothpaste, used checkbooks and a box of emery boards. That is, until last week. I was having trouble balancing my checkbook. I was three months in arrears with this task and had to have it complete in fifteen minutes before the bank closed.

I pulled out the blinking wonder and began to push the mechanical numbers with general abandonment. In three minutes, I had not only balanced my checkbook, but added up all the pictures in the house, figured out a can't-possibly-fail way to get rich and planned our retirement.

I don't think I'll ever recover. Now I find myself looking for ways and reasons to use my calculator. I knew things would never be the same yesterday when I refused to leave my desk for six hours until my adding machine had recharged itself. I was determined to figure out how many hours I would save in a lifetime by using my calculator.

26

Keeping the Checkbook

If I had my way I would never let anyone see my checkbook. It isn't that I do a poor job. It's that I know no one could ever appreciate the fine art involved in keeping ahead of the bank with my checks.

Several weeks ago Frank decided that it was time for a periodic checkbook check-up. I tried to make all my notations and studs plain and readable.

The first stub had a finely scrawled note, "Call Inez."

"Why did you write this note here, Linda? The checkbook is not the place for notes. It is a written account of the checks and deposits we have made through our bank."

"Well, that was a very important note," I explained. "It concerned a check we had written on the twenty-first of the month to the church. I had to call Inez to see how much the check was made out for."

"The purpose of the check stub is to tell how much the check was written for, dear," Frank said, gritting out a smile.

"Oh, I couldn't use that stub because I had already used all the lines on it for the check which I had written to the church the week before. Then I couldn't remember whether I had paid the entire amount to the church or spread it out to the missionaries we help support and send money to each month. It's really very simple."

Then flipping over to the ninth stub I showed Frank a carefully erased and penciled stub. "See, I put the final total on this stub. Then I subtracted the deposit I made on Monday."

"Wait a minute," Frank interrupted. "You subtracted the deposit. You're supposed to add your deposits."

"No, I had to subtract this deposit because I had added it on check stub No. 459. Only I added too much. Then when I actually made the deposit, I found we only had $94 instead of $194 available. So I had to subtract the deposit."

"Then we have $100 in bad checks floating around somewhere."

"Honey, I wouldn't do that," I explained patiently. "You see, I haven't mailed five of the checks out yet. They're sitting right in the kitchen."

"Where are they?" Frank inquired.

"They're here. Where I put all my bills which are waiting to be mailed. Right here in the mixing bowls."

"Okay. Then we aren't in the hole. You didn't mail out but $94 in checks.

"Oh, no. I explain right here in the checkbook. I mailed out $124. The insurance payment had to be paid this week."

"Then we're in the hole $30."

"Honey, just listen. I can explain it all. We aren't in the red. See, it's all plainly written on check stub No. 510. I took the $40 which I keep in the bank as extra which is not added to the amount in the checkbook, but it is in the bank. So I added it to the amount shown on the stub. See, it's always there in the bank. I just don't show it. Then I subtracted the insurance bill from that."

"Linda, let me ask you one question. Do we have any money in the bank?"

"Oh, yes, we have $20 total. There is the $10 shown on the check stubs. Then there is the $10 emergency fund. I don't ever add the emergency fund to the total except in an emergency, of course."

"That's all right, Linda," Frank said walking away from the dining room table. "I'm going into the family room. I want you to work on the checkbook. Then when you have it straight and in order, call me in. I'll check it over then."

I sat there staring at him as he left the room. How could he possibly not understand the simple rudiments of accounting? Just as he rounded the corner into the family room, I called to him, "I'm sorry, dear. I don't think it will do any good to work on my checkbook any more. See, either you understand accounting or you don't. There's just no middle of the road."

27

The Sewing Lessons

There is an old saying. "A little knowledge is a dangerous thing." I didn't know how dangerous until I took sewing lessons.

For years I knew almost nothing about sewing. Yet I was a prolific seamstress. Then I took my sewing lessons. I had kept both girls in summer and winter wardrobes. I also had sewed for both myself and Frank. I had just graduated to men's pants and ties. I sewed double-knit pants until his closets bulged. My specialty became men's ties. Frank's tie rack became so overburdened with all my figured and fancy ties that we had to enlarge the closet. Then I decided the thing I needed to do was take sewing lessons.

I have not sewn one stitch since.

In the class were three dress designers, four professional sewing class attenders, a high fashion model who made her own clothes, three sewing teachers and me.

Now all I knew about sewing was what I had read on the Simplicity Easy-to-Sew patterns. I knew what a dart and a seam were. After that I was lost.

For the first class I proudly wore the new outfit I had made from scrap upholstery material. The teacher used me as her model that day. She found ninety-three drastic mistakes I had made on the left sleeve. I didn't wear anything I had made again to the class. Since I had made most of my clothes that meant I had to go out and buy a ready-made wardrobe.

During the class I found out what a pleat was. I found out , how to sew away from corners in order to keep that horrible pucker from forming. I saw how to obtain the professional look in all my dresses by not ironing the hems.

The wealth of information I learned has made me the greatest sewing critic in the world. I can now look at any homemade outfit and instantly detect misplaced darts, baggy shoulders and upside-down buttons. I can give the price and type of material and where it was purchased. Of course, I would never dare sew another garment myself.

I know now that I am completely inadequate for all sewing tasks. I even send my buttons out to a professional to be sewn on properly. I would not tackle a hem unless I were threatened with no fudge for a week.

I am appalled that for ten years or more I was so dumb that I didn't know that I was not qualified to sew. Even more appalling is the fact that there were sewing critics in every material shop in town who could recognize a garment I had made from my sewing errors. I found out that to walk into one of those shops opens you to scrutiny and analyzation. With my errors that was disastrous.

I learned many things during my sewing class and one important Christian principle was reinforced. The New Testament teaches that we are to walk in the light as we have the light. That means, of course, that we can only act in the area that God has opened to our understanding. Many times with infant Christians I've been like my sewing critics. Unjustly I've judged their mistakes and failures by my years of walking with the Lord.

Because I was raised in a Christian home, some hard-learned principles of discipline were ingrained at an early age.

The fearful anticipation of sewing class I had must've been experienced by many of my friends when they've encountered my critical eye of scrutiny.

I hope they've learned to send their failures out to the only professional failure fixer, Jesus. He can take the criticism we heap on each other and turn it into steps toward righteousness.

28

The Never-Ending Story
of Gilligan's Island

Gilligan's Island is a program which was on television when I was a teenager. I have been watching it for twenty years.

It comes on in the afternoon at five o'clock, five-thirty and six o'clock. The children watch it three times a day. They have kept this grueling schedule for the past three years. Since that's the time I'm cooking supper in the kitchen which adjoins the family room, I have to watch too.

I can recite whole segments of the actions. Not only that but given the first line in several of the shows I can give you all the dialogue, describe in detail the sets, describe the exact expressions on each actor's face, giving lighting positions and camera angles.

I have never watched Gilligan's Island by choice. But along with the Lord's sustaining love and the air they breathe, my children can't live without at least two segments of Gilligan's Island each day.

The other afternoon I decided that I had had it. "Turn off the television or change the channel," I instructed Leah. "I can't stand another day with the Professor and Mary Ann."

"But, mother," Leah said bursting into tears, "I can't turn this one off. I've only seen it two times and it's my favorite one. It's the one about Mary Ann and Gilligan. They almost fall in love and fall off the cliff instead."

"Leah," I said in amazement. "You know that you've seen that one at least twenty times."

"Well, I've seen it only twice this week. Oh, please, mother, please don't make me turn it off."

"All right. If it means that much to you, you can watch it."

I started supper while Leah settled down contentedly mouthing each word of the dialogue.

Television for the American housewife is a fact of life. Even if you don't have TV in your home, fashions, peer groups, politics, government and almost every other area in our society is influenced by the oval tube.

Though I don't want to watch many of the older rerun programs myself, I've found at times they can be a reinforcement to spiritual principles we've tried to teach the children. When the point taken is one we may disagree with, it provides an open door to express our views on an issue.

Close censureship, of course, is necessary. Our home is the dwelling place for the Lord. Not everything is suitable for the family to see, but there is no need to pour out the clean clothes with the wash water.

The Bible shows that all creation is made for our benefit. It's hard for me to believe, but that can even include Gilligan's Island.

29

What Happens
to All the Hangers

What happens to all our clothes hangers? Either there is a monumental conspiracy perpetrated by some vicious villain or there is a clothes hanger-eating monster that lives in our closets.

There is nothing more disturbing to a housewife than to have a fresh load of clothes ready for the closets and no hangers. My routine for putting up clothes is to adorn myself with my clean sparkling goodies. I drape them from every protruding point on my body. My fingers, both arms, ears and nose are covered and adorned. Cautiously and with great care I make my way to the bedroom where I am supposed to find hangers for my clean clothes. Alas, there is never a hanger to be found.

Several months ago Frank searched for twenty-four hours for one hanger just to put up his coat. Finally he put his coat back on and ran over to the nearest department store. He bought out their entire stock of coat hangers.

Things went well for all of us for about two weeks. Then

slowly the prized bent-brass beauties began to disintegrate and disappear again.

In college my husband was called the "clothes hanger engineer." It was because he could make anything from a hanger: mobiles, lighting fixtures, transistor radios, table tops and even Brunswick stew. Our children have inherited their father's adept fingers for clothes hanger design. Their index fingers have permanent dents which match perfectly the neck of a clothes hanger where it is twisted to shape. They can dismantle a closet full of hangers in thirty seconds.

We are the only family on the block who has stoves, surfboards, sewing machines, chairs and a refrigerator repaired with clothes hangers.

The other day I walked into my son's room. He was draped over his bed reading. "Have you seen any clothes hangers?" I asked cautiously.

"Yeah," he replied proudly. "I looked all over the house and finally found one."

"Let me use it to hang up this shirt," I said.

"Sorry, mother, you're too late. I've put it to use already."

"Well, whatever you hung on it, take it down. This is your father's new shirt. I need a clothes hanger for it. I want it to be hung neatly."

"I can't. You're too late. There it is." Sitting on his dresser was a small, modern art statue of a man playing the french horn. "See. I used it for my project I had to do for band."

Am I wrong to feel as though there's nothing which can stop the clothes hanger villains who live in our house? It doesn't matter a lot though. In God's economy, I know creative imagination put to work in statues and repaired refrigerators is more important than hangers any day.

30

My New Recipes

Since I almost never allow more than thirty minutes to prepare supper, I have come up with some of the most interesting new dishes. Not all of them are good to eat but all of them are interesting.

In an attempt to make my family, especially the children, appreciate them, I give them all a name. At first I entitled all my new recipes, "Surprise" something. There was Surprise Beef, Surprise Eggs, Surprise Pork, Surprise Vegetables. Then the children caught on. "Oh, no. Not another recipe you made up," they would whine.

So, I changed my titles. They all became "Desperation" dishes. After Desperation Salad and Desperation Stew came that familiar, "Oh, you made it up," whine.

I have decided that I will quit trying to hide the fact that I've made up the terrific new recipes we often have for supper. Now whenever I've whipped up something out of my head, I put a sign on the door which I had printed for the occasion. It reads: Before you ask, we're having something new, different and delicious. It is a culinary treat made in the time honored tradition of Surprise Beef and Desperation Stew.

"What, may I ask, is the matter with experimenting with food to come up with great dishes to serve our family?" I recently asked my husband. We were having a quiet lunch together. I had prepared my supreme and ultimate gourmet dish, peasant salad.

"Nothing," Frank mumbled, through puckered, slightly parted lips. "You know I enjoy everything you cook. There's only one question though, Linda. Who put glue in the food?"

31

The Never-Fail Fudge

I have several "never-fail" recipes. I've a whole collection of them, in fact. One is called Never-Fail Fudge. The only problem is, it never fails to fail.

I have eaten enough fudge with a spoon and saucer to cover the Empire State Building. I know one woman who got so tired of eating her Never-Fail Fudge this way that she began using it as a sandwich spread.

At first I thought that the reason it always failed was because I added my own variations to it. Therefore, I wrote in bold red letters across the face of the recipe, "Do not use this recipe unless you plan to follow all the directions."

Unfortunately that didn't work. In fact it seemed to get harder when I was adding raisins, oatmeal and sunflower seeds to it.

I decided on another plan of attack. I would cook it a little longer. Instead of the recommended three minutes, I would cook it until I felt it had gotten to the right consistency. I cooked one batch for five hours and fifteen minutes. It not only didn't get hard but it tasted like runny rubber.

I'm always embarrassed when the children bring home notes from their school which read, "We will have a homemade candy sale this week. Please send a batch of fudge with your child to school Tuesday."

One day I called Leah's teacher and asked, "How do you recommend Leah carry this fudge?"

"Oh, she can bring it in a paper bag," was the professional, quick reply.

"Fat chance," I said under my breath.

The next Tuesday, Leah trotted off to school with a batch of my Never-Fail Fudge in a paper bag. I got a phone call from the principal twenty minutes later. Leah was facing suspension for maliciously vandalizing the school.

The fudge had leaked through the bag and smeared all over the sidewalk. It somehow creeped into four lockers, got into the hair of seven first graders and three teachers. As though that were not enough, the assistant principal's office had to be closed. He had gone home to change his clothes.

Leah had innocently gone into his office to ask special permission to enter the school early to use the bathroom to wash the fudge off her hands and legs. The bag had continued to leak. The assistant principal had come into his office and slipped on the sticky goo.

Fortunately, he had not been injured. His desk and office, however, had been almost totally destroyed.

I shall keep trying though. It doesn't matter what anyone may think. If it says "never fail," it's got to be never fail.

32

It's Wash
and Wear Or . . .

The other night we were out to supper with some friends. The men settled down to engineering conversation. Gwen and I started to talk about a publisher she writes for who is compiling a book for women on household tips. "Do you have any laundry, ironing or cooking tips you can pass on?" my friend inquired.

I chuckled, "I have a great ironing tip, but I doubt that they would want it in their book."

I have adapted for my own use a tip I received from a neighbor. One day we were at her house. She was folding clothes. She came to a wrinkled shirt. It looked worn and frayed but still usable. She tossed it into the rag bag. "Around here," she said, "it's either wash and wear or wash and throw out."

Now I don't advocate throwing out clothes. But there is a principle involved here. I have found there is a way you can end all your ironing. It comes from careful label examination. Never, never, even under threat of life or a five hundred calorie diet, buy anything unless it is permanent press. I totally disregard style, size or cost of any garment I plan to purchase. All I look at is the washing label.

I've learned that unless you have the eagle eye of a jail warden and the mind of a supreme court judge, you can be trapped by deceiving washing labels.

Some of them read, "Almost no ironing." Don't buy it. That means your garment will come out of the dryer looking like a saltine cracker.

Another label may say, "May require light, warm iron touch up." Don't buy it. In simple language it says, "There is no way under the blue sky you can possibly get all the wrinkles out. You can iron until your electricity bill is $3,435, but you will not get them out."

Only wash and wear labels are safe. The one which says, "Never, never requires ironing," is the only one I ever buy.

Too often as a Christian, I've made the mistake of looking at the labels of my friends and relatives in the same way.

When the Lord touched our family about twelve years ago with a fresh work from the Holy Spirit, we found that our labels suddenly changed. Because we were no longer wash and wear, some of the people we knew were ready to throw us out of their Christian circles.

With a renewed zeal and joy, we didn't care a lot about what they thought anyway. We were perfectly content to let our labels become a barrier to love.

Years have come and gone and we have seen the Lord do some real miracles in our lives. The working of the Lord is always what changes minds and hearts. Our experiences haven't made us flaming fanatics but more stable in the love of Jesus. Surer that we are His.

Other lives are touched, their labels either wiped away or

lost. Once again, God is allowing us to have our labels become a point of communication with many of our fellow Christians.

Instead of hearing, "You know I can't possibly accept you because of that doctrine," we are hearing more and more, "Let me tell you what great thing the Lord has done."

In clothes, labels make a tremendous difference. With God's children, they are less than important.

33

Underwear Repentance

Frank has finally gotten used to women stopping him in the church to ask if he has on clean underwear. I really had no idea what far-reaching results my sharing the story of underwear repentance would have.

I was teaching a class of women about a year ago. I had to illustrate repentance. The most clear-cut case of repentance which had happened to me in recent years involved Frank's underwear.

In all our married life, I had not been able to keep underwear and socks in Frank's bureau drawer. I tried. It seemed that I would spend the whole day washing, drying and putting away clothes only to find in the morning that Frank had no underwear to put on. He would have to sing the same old song learned over the years, "Are there any underwear in the dryer?" I would make a mad dash to the garage praying, "Lord, just let there be one pair, please."

I became a great runner with tremendous leg muscles, but my problem with Frank's underwear remained unresolved.

He never had any in his drawer. It was almost as though there were a cotton demon who lived in there and ate, devoured, destroyed and dirtied his undershirts and pants.

One night I became completely distraught. It was after midnight. I had crawled into bed tired and almost asleep. Suddenly I was wide awake. Frank's underwear! Did he have any? I looked in his drawer and, of course, his drawer was empty.

I took several pair out of the clothes hamper and took them to the machine to wash. Propping my eyelids open with spray starch, I decided I had to pray. This underwear problem had to be resolved once and forever.

"Lord, I repent of never having clean underwear for Frank," I prayed. "I promise to do better."

"Wait a minute, Linda," the Lord spoke to my heart. "That's not true repentance."

"What do you mean? I said I would do better."

"That's just the point. Linda, when you accepted me as your Savior and Lord, did you promise to do better or to be better?"

"No. I knew I couldn't be any better. I looked to your mercy to clean up my life."

"That's right," the Lord reassured me. "But you did become a better person, didn't you? You were changed. You did the repenting. I did the changing. I'm God, not you. If I can keep your life clean, don't you think I can keep undershirts clean?"

"Okay, Lord," I prayed, "I repent. I'm not promising anything. I turn myself over to your mercy and grace."

God's grace is sufficient even for underwear. From that night on, Frank's drawers have been bulging with underwear. I can't believe it. Some nights, I go through the same old panic. "Oh, no," I wonder. "Does Frank have underwear?" I'll check and there is always enough there.

I don't completely understand it. My routine didn't seem to change any. I am not working nearly as hard at keeping underwear in his drawer. They are simply there whenever he needs them.

Only once or maybe twice in two years has Frank been without a clean undershirt or socks.

I rejoice each time I open his drawer and see those shiny, white, clean cotton jockeys. Frank can always assure inquirers that God is faithful and, yes, he has clean underwear.

Believe me, if God can work with underwear repentance, He can work with any kind of repentance. The formula is simple. We do the repenting. He does the changing.

34

My Marvelous Washday Schedule

My friend, Mrs. Clean, says that each month she goes through her closets and drawers and rewashes everything.

This seems to be only a slight variation of my own washing methods. I wash once a month, never before.

I learned this clever washday trick over a period of years. I started this plan quite by accident about ten years ago.

Like most other housewives, I was caught in the everyday wash cycle. One day I came across an enterprising young mother of five children who said she washed only once a week. "That's for me." My eyes glowed as I rubbed both hands together.

How could she manage to wash only once a week was my first question.

"Easy," she said. "You just buy enough underwear to last for a week. Then you replace them one at a time as they wear out. The initial outlay of cash is the only additional expense."

I ran immediately to my local department store and in breathless excitement purchased enough undies to last a week for my husband, children and myself.

Once I had caught on to the once-a-week washing cycle it was easy to stretch it into two weeks, three weeks. Now I have finally reached the utopia of the laundry world. I wash once a month.

My present schedule is actually an outgrowth of the recent energy crisis. Conservation of electricity and water being my main concern, I patriotically pushed my washing schedule to the first day of the month.

I know some clinically clean cynics will question how this is possible. My methods are simple and direct. I never throw away any clothes. I keep all clothes because no matter how worn or ragged they may be, they will eventually be needed.

But the real secret lies in the fact that in our house, nothing is considered dirty until it has been worn several times.

Mornings in our home go something like this: "Mother, have you washed my blue dress with purple people heads?"

I casually glance from my daily Bible readings, "Now, dear, you know this is only the fifteenth. Washday isn't for two weeks."

"But, mom, I need that dress for school."

"Where is it?" I ask warily. "You didn't put it in the dirty clothes hamper, did you? You know that monster digests almost everything you put in it."

"Yes, of course, I put it in the dirty clothes hamper. It was dirty."

"What do you mean it was dirty? You had only worn it seven times. You know nothing is dirty until it has been worn at least ten times. Where is your patriotism? Have you gotten these communist ideas from your social studies class at school?"

"Mother! I need that dress."

"Wear something else," I reply, turning back to my Bible.

"I don't have anything else."

"What do you mean? You have a closet full of good clothes."

"All I have is one dress left and I haven't been able to wear it since kindergarten graduation."

Ah, but the day I wash becomes a celebration. Everyone in the household finds lost possessions and forgotten clothing.

"My petrified rock! I left it in my jeans. Oh, thanks, mom."

"My blue dress!"

"My comb!"

My husband's comment is usually a plaintive and weary sigh, "Clean shirts."

Unfortunately every plan has one small flaw. My once-a-month washday plan does have at least one drawback. We never seem to have any clean clothes in the house.

35

She's Two Years Old and Still Not Housebroken

Naomi is two years old now. She has grown into a beautiful young dog. She wags her tail lovingly. She barks at the right times. She doesn't bark at the right times. She is an absolute lady about almost everything. There is one large flaw in her sterling character though.

She still is not housebroken. I would take any advice offered. I am open to any and all suggestions. My friend, Dee, reassuringly patted me on the head one day and said, "Don't worry about it. Some people can train dogs and some can't. You're one of the can'ts. Accept it as a fact of life and keep the dog outside."

In self-defense in the last few months, I have had to follow her advice. Up until that time I had scrubbed my carpet so many times, I have permanent high and low carpet patterns on my knees and the top of my feet. One spot in the living room is the favorite place for her accidents. The color has changed from a brown to a sick yellow from all the disinfectant and goop I've used trying to get rid of the odor.

We've sprinkled black pepper on the rugs to discourage her. That was a sure remedy we were told. No dog will have an accident unless she can sniff out the place first. The black pepper eliminates the sniffing and therefore accidents are also eliminated. Naomi either has an asbestos nose or she has her accidents without sniffing. The black pepper only worked on a few small children who tried to crawl on the carpet.

We've spent enough money on remedies and housebreaking cures to completely outfit a child for a year and pay for a set of dental braces. Still she must remain outside.

Several nights ago we had a friend for dinner. While I served the dessert I explained to him our problems with Naomi. "Sh-h-h-h," our friend said. "She may hear you."

"Well, what difference does that make?" I asked in hushed tones.

"She has definitely developed a psychosis about this problem. You must treat her with great tenderness and love. Don't let her sense your disapproval. Then she'll get over it in no time at all. Believe me. I know what I'm talking about. If you give her the love and understanding which is due a sensitive young animal, she will reward you with obedience to your slightest wish."

"That's it," I said gleefully. "I have repressed and suppressed her long enough. I have abandoned her to the back yard making her feel unloved and unwanted."

"Now, you have the right spirit," our friend agreed.

I rushed out to bring Naomi into the house. I petted and caressed her. "You may have free rein of the house. Run and play," I said to her in loving proud tones.

The next morning after a night of freedom throughout the house, Naomi went back into the yard. I spent the rest of the day scrubbing the carpets.

I've gone back to Dee's advice. Some people can train dogs and some can't. I'm one of the can'ts. I'll just love Naomi from her permanent home, the back yard.

God isn't like that with us, however. He has never ending patience in teaching us His ways.

He took forty years in the wilderness to train Moses. By the time God was finished, Moses was able to lead the stiff-necked, rebellious children of Israel out of Egypt and through the wilderness for another forty years.

Even if I continue to make a mess out of my life and work, God is patient to give me a second, a third, a fourth chance.

Many years ago, I overheard a conversation between two ministers. One was a young man, fiery and alert. The other was bent, old and slow. They were discussing a colleague who had fallen into an immoral affair with a woman. Even though he knew that he was in sin, he seemed powerless to control himself.

"How many times do I have to put up with that man's backsliding ways. He has been back time and time again. I minister to him and pour out my best efforts to him. I'll tell you now I'm tired of his inconsistent way." The younger minister was firmly beating a fist into his other hand to punctuate each sentence. "How many times do I have to minister to this man?" He asked again to give emphasis to his question.

The older man straightened his bent body and quietly whispered, "You should minister to him as many times as he comes back for help."

Sometimes I can mentally see a picture of Satan accusing me before the Lord God. Jesus then turns to His Father and calmly says, "She might be twenty-five years old in our family and not housebroken, but she should have another chance. After all, I died for her."

When it comes to training a dog, I may have to live with being one of the can'ts, but I'm thankful God can train His children in the way He wants them to go.

36

The Telephone

I'm a "telephoneholic." The telephone is to me what coffee, cigarettes and booze are to some others. Every day at least one friend will call and say, "You're the hardest person in the world to get in touch with. Are any of your conversations under an hour in length?"

"Not many," I truthfully say. Then I coyly and cunningly lure my prey and fellow telephone talker into a forty-five minute conversation. I'm the woman you've read about in all those cartoons and jokes who talks for fifteen minutes before she discovers it's a wrong number.

Don't try to put any condemnation on me though. I'm through taking it from people. The telephone for a mother with small children is a main road to other adult voices and sanity. My idea of having lunch with a friend is to eat a peanut butter and jelly sandwich in the middle of a noon time telephone conversation.

At the beginning of the school year a friend of mine called one morning. "I'm free!" she yelled in my ear. "Ted started first grade. Now I can begin to go places, do things again. I won't have to imagine what a person looks like when I talk with them. I can talk face to face. Do you realize it's been six years since I've had that freedom?"

"Don't gloat," I said scornfully. "It's been thirteen years for me and I'm still not free."

"Well, I won't be calling you much any more. I won't have too much time. I've joined a Bible study, a prayer group, a bowling league, and I plan to take up tennis. But do you think I could come over and see you sometime? Maybe I could even come this morning."

"Oh, that would be wonderful. Would you?"

At eleven o'clock, an attractive, vaguely familiar young woman knocked on my door.

I cracked it open. "Yes?" I asked.

"Linda, don't you recognize me?"

"The voice is definitely one I know, but I can't place your face."

"It's me, Irene. We talk every day on the phone."

"Oh, Irene. Come in. Oh, yes, please come in."

Irene didn't stay long. We didn't have much to say to each other. It seems that I can't carry on a decent conversation unless I have the telephone cord wrapped around my legs and a heavy object shaped like a receiver balanced between my ear and shoulder.

It doesn't matter though. Soon after she left, the phone rang. An unknown weak female voice squeaked, "Hello, anyone. Is there anybody out there?"

It was the mother of a three-year-old son and a one-month-old daughter. We talked for three hours and twenty-one minutes. We exchanged recipes, antidotes, birthdays, pattern numbers and experiences.

The Telephone

She calls every day now.

Each night when I count the blessings the Lord has bountifully given us, the telephone is right there near the top. I place it just after my salvation, husband and children.

37

The Clever Disguise

Underneath the clever disguise I've devised for my house, there is a spotlessly clean mausoleum. I keep it in disguise, however, for several reasons.

I find that no one is comfortable in an overly immaculate, shining house. They are always afraid they will spill something, spot the rug or put a dent in the coffee table.

Not at our house. The decor of our home includes three large brown spots on our olive green carpet. Our coffee tables are appropriately scarred and scraped in order to make anyone realize that it's perfectly all right to put their cup of tea down on it.

Much of the joy of our Christianity comes from having people in for dinner and coffee. We find the Lord can break down many barriers over a good dinner and conversation. But no one wants to be interrupted by a Clean Jean or Molly Mop-up who is continually dusting and rearranging the knickknacks.

Therefore, we have adopted the "lived-in" policy. We try

to keep the homey lived-in appearance while still maintaining enough order to keep the health department away.

I also find that it gives many of my overly zealous nervous homemaker friends something to do with their hands while visiting our home.

They can always find a few shriveled peas hidden in the carpet or behind a chair. They pick up their prize and then waltz to the trash can delighted. Once they have found my secretly placed pea, they immediately begin their cautious clean-up caper. They start slowly at first. They simply pick up our tea cups and take them to the kitchen. Once in the kitchen, they pick up steam. They are soon dusting the furniture and sweeping the floors. They can spend a delightful hour or two ministering to my needs.

We part with both parties satisfied and happy. My friends have had an opportunity to apply their particular ministry on my house. I wind up with an immaculate living room, clean dishes and sparkling light fixtures.

In the Old Testament, Abraham's wife Sarah knew this principle in housekeeping. When three angels came for a midday visit, she stopped all her household chores to oversee their needs. Paul says that there may be times when we will be serving angels though we don't even know it.

For years I lived in a special fear. I had visions that one day someone would show up at my door and the house wouldn't be straight and tidy.

I prayed daily that I wouldn't be embarrassed by drop-in, unexpected guests. God always honored my prayer until one day about three years ago.

A friend appeared at eight o'clock one bright, clear Monday morning. I didn't have my eyes open much less have the house clean. She roamed through our cluttered rooms laughingly making snide remarks about the lousy condition of the house.

Much to my surprise, I laughed too.

After she left and I was at last straightening up, the still voice of the Lord began to tenderly probe my heart. "Linda," I felt Him say, "you've always feared that someone would one day catch your house in this condition."

That was certainly right. Now it had happened. My friend had even made fun of me and accused me of being the world's lousiest housekeeper.

I had to admit to myself and the Lord that I was surprised at my own reaction. I wasn't embarrassed or hurt or even angry. I felt a sense of relief.

From that day on, I've turned my house over to Jesus to do with it what He will. Oh, we had had a dedication service in our home years before, but I became willing to let the Lord dictate who will show up and when. Now there seems to be a steady stream of people in and out. We laugh, talk, praise, pray.

Many days the house is draped in her clever disguise, but the people don't stop coming.

One day I may take my house out of her disguise. I may also become a Molly Mop-up. But in the meantime, we shall enjoy our home and live in it. For now there are too many delightful Christians we want to get to know. Too many sunsets to bask in. Too many friends with nervous fingers who delight in helping with the mess.

38

My Friend

I'm a sucker for almost any activity which involves a group of women. My reputation for enjoying Tupperware parties once earned me the honor of being invited to four parties in one week. Whether it be Sarah Coventry, a plant party or just a plain coffee klatsch I want to be there.

One of God's greatest gifts to the human race is a friend. Jesus said to His disciples, "I'm going to be your friend from now on." He knew the value of a good friend.

Catherine was my friend. Almost every afternoon I would mosey over to her house. I never intended to stay long but the minutes always melted into an hour or two. One cup of tea became three.

I'm not sure what she believed about Jesus. I don't think I ever gave her a chance to tell me. I was much too busy telling her about her need for Him. As much as I tried to intimidate her, I could never push her into becoming as zealous about the Lord as I wanted her to be.

But I loved Catherine and she loved me. I know she was

my friend because she put up with my endless badgering.

Then Catherine moved back home to Massachusetts. I still miss her. Oh, not every day but quiet times, soft times I remember and pray for her.

Several years ago she wrote in a Christmas card to us, "Praise the Lord! Don't worry about me, Linda. God hasn't given up yet. My mother badgers me now almost as much as you would if you were here."

Catherine and Jesus have a lot in common. They put up with me just as I am because they love me and because they're my friends.

39

Heavenly Rubs

It seems to me that certain people have been put in the Body of Christ for one primary purpose—to bug me. I have heard all kinds of spiritual explanations for this phenomenon. They all sound so good until that brother or sister who is my spiritual sandpaper comes close enough to rub me.

Then all I want to do is fight and spar. For days after each encounter, I come under terrible condemnation for my unhealed reactions.

Recently, however, I have come to the conclusion that perhaps it's not all my fault. God may want to change something in my brothers and sisters.

One woman who is sandpaper for me is on a continual spiritual high. She is sure that if I'm not flying somewhere at the spiritual altitude of 30,000 feet I am doomed to a fate worse than death. I get tired of flapping and flying all the time. I have to come down occasionally. There is nothing like a valley between mountain peaks in order to catch up with my reading, naps and housecleaning.

Then there is another woman who is an expert on every subject in the Bible. She has experienced everything, done everything, seen everything, been everywhere and knows everyone. This woman is especially irritating to me because she is so much like me.

Even with my wealth of knowledge I have to admit every once in a while, I just don't have all the answers. I also get tired of having so many good answers only to have people go away again and again without a solution to their problems. It has made me think that my pat replies may not really be the answer God wants to give. Maybe some answers can only come from Jesus, the Author and Finisher of our faith.

I have had people demand that I cut my hair, leave it long, wear it up, take it down, scramble my eggs, eat them raw. It always seems that my salvation or something as crucial depends on my following the advice of my sandpaper.

For a year I had a dear woman who called me every day so we could argue about something. I thought I was hiding my irritation pretty well. Finally just before she moved out of town, she confided in me, "We really haven't gotten along too well, have we? Do you think we shouldn't have talked to each other so much?"

I don't think that the answer to the problem is isolation. Isolation from a problem doesn't make a problem go away. God deliberately puts people who rub and irritate in my path in order to change me.

Yet I'm convinced there is another reason too. The Lord has allowed them to cross my path to give these brothers and sisters someone to pray for them. You see, the things which bug me about them are always glaring faults in my own personality. Therefore I can pray for them with added awareness and understanding.

When I face the fact that my friend has a problem and that it's a problem I probably share with her, new vision and growth is worked in my heart.

Could it be God really has put certain people in my path for one primary purpose—to bug me?

40

The Difference Is Jesus

"There was a freight train which came by our apartment in the middle of the night. I can remember sitting on the cold floor crying while it passed."

Somehow my friend and I had started talking about her first marriage and what her life had been like before she met Jesus.

The nightmare of this alcoholic, brutal man and a lonely, lost young woman filled the living room and began to envelop us.

My friend rearranged the couch pillows and sighed a deep breath, "So one day he decided to knock some sense into me. It wasn't the first time he had beaten me. I guess that time he finally did knock me back to my senses. In the morning I left him."

Just then the back door flew open and a ray of sunlight burst in the door.

"Mommy, will you pray for my leg? I hurt myself."

A short, brown body ran to the couch. "Sure, babe, where

does it hurt?

"Father, in Jesus' name, heal this leg."

"Thank you, Jesus," the brown ray of sunlight called as he ran for the door.

"Hallelujah!" my friend said in reply as the back door closed.

Not another word was said. Words would have only spoiled that delightful knowing between friends. Our smiles and joy said it far more eloquently than any talk could ever say, "What a difference Jesus makes."

41

Our Narrow Escape With the Police

Several years ago Frank was the youth director of our church. We decided one Halloween night to invite all the young people over to the house for a special party. Several teenage pranks had been pulled in our community the year before on Halloween. The police were going to be on the prowl for all older teenagers who were out getting into trouble.

The young people arrived early. The first indication that they were there was a tremendous thud on the roof. Four of them had climbed on top of the house and were holding a square dance. We had no sooner gotten them down than we heard strange eerie sounds coming from the closet. Two had come over about four-thirty in the afternoon. They had been hiding, undetected, in different parts of the house for two hours.

We knew that they were in a good humor when one of the boys poured Tabasco sauce in the punch and then graciously poured me a full glass.

Things went from low chaos to semi-riot. They were lighting sparklers in the car, popping water balloons throughout the house and playing tag with my hibiscus bushes.

Some of them had come dressed in costume. One boy was dressed in a black Johnny Cash type outfit complete with a BB gun. We had told them that almost anything was fair game, just stay in our yard. They had been obedient which was most unfortunate for our lawn.

About eight-thirty we called them all inside. The special speaker for the night had arrived. Our guest saw the young people were a bit keyed up and immediately called them to prayer. They calmed down quickly.

A knock came at the door.

I answered it. I was in costume. I had on a blonde straw wig with Frank's pants and shirt stuffed with pillows. I had a couple of front teeth blackened and freckles painted on my cheeks. Standing at the door was a stern and official policeman.

"May I speak to the lady of the house?" he said.

"I'm the lady of the house," I quivered.

"I understand you're having a wild party over here. There was a report that someone had a rifle."

"Come in, officer," I said beckoning him into the family room where a group of angelic young people were assembled praying.

"I see I have the wrong house or something," he said, apologetically surveying the room.

"Oh, no, officer, this may be the place. The young people were a bit wound up a few minutes ago. But as you can see, everything is under control."

"Listen, lady," the policeman said taking off his hat in

reverence. "I didn't want to interrupt your prayer meeting. It was a crank call, I'm sure. Yet we do have to check out these things."

"It's quite all right, sir," I said. "I appreciate your concern."

The officer left scratching his head.

Only God could have turned that unruly group into angelic glows just in the nick of time.

On occasion we're ignorant of the problem we may be causing others or how we may look. I'm glad God has so much mercy that He often hides our failures from others. What the world sees many times is not the chaos or semi-riot but angelic faces of calm.

When Roger went to Brazil for a short missionary trip several years ago, he left his wife Ramona and their two girls in the States. Ramona was immediately thrown into a whirlwind of speaking engagements, housekeeping and mounting responsibility. Shortly before Christmas, she became very ill and had to be confined to bed. Her doctor's diagnosis was complete exhaustion.

The morning before Thanksgiving, she struggled out of bed and went shopping, determined to make the holiday pleasant for the girls while their father was away. I saw her while she was in the grocery store. She looked worn and drawn. She smiled weakly at me as I passed her and two other women who were carrying on a rapid conversation with this poor limp dishrag of a woman.

As I was looking over the meat, the two women were at the same counter. "Have you ever seen Ramona looking better," asked the short, older lady. "She gets younger every day."

"You know she had that conversion experience several years ago," the other one said in a hushed tone. "I think she has gotten prettier each time I see her. There is a new light in her eyes now."

I almost giggled in the hamburger. How could it be that these women had not seen the pale, drawn expression on Ramona's face? I knew how ill she was. Yet the Lord had hidden that from these women. They had seen radiance, charm and grace. God's love had shown through her weakened condition and touched two hearts.

Looking into the family room at the prayerful young saints that Halloween night, I breathed a thankful prayer of relief for our narrow escape with the police and for a God who sometimes chooses to hide our failures.

42

I Can't Get Home With the Butterflies

There are many mysteries in this world I don't think I'll ever understand. One is the position of the stars. Then there are the tides, new life, the size and splendor of the universe.

One other mystery is: Why can't I ever get home from the store with eight matching glasses?

For Christmas, Carol gave me a beautiful set of glassware. They had doves positioned in a tiffany type setting. They were hand painted in blacks and reds. Because I didn't buy them or bring them into the house, they made the journey intact. They didn't make it in one piece through the month of January, however. Even though I only used them one time, by February we were down to two doves.

Undaunted I went to the store to buy some more. The gift shop was out of dove glasses. I had to settle for butterflies. I took it all rather well and cheerfully bought the butterflies.

I had another errand to run before I came home. I walked into the house triumphant. "Guess what!" I said to Frank.

"It must be something good. We got a check for one

thousand dollars in the mail."

"No. Better than that." I reached into my shopping bag and pulled out the new glasses. "We now have eight matching glasses. Count them. Eight matching glasses."

"I only count six," Frank said unimpressed. "Two of them are broken."

I couldn't believe my eyes. Two of the beautiful butterflies were crushed to bits.

"Can't you ever get glasses home without breaking them?" Frank asked.

Ignoring his question, I toyed with the idea of taking them back to the store as defective. After all, anyone should be able to get glasses home without having them break. I threw the idea out though when I remembered the time I broke a guaranteed indestructible plastic shampoo bottle. It was the kind they tossed around on ceramic floors in the television commercials. I knew it couldn't be faulty manufacturing which broke those delicate butterflies. It was I.

"Frank," I pleaded, "I can't go back to that store and get more glasses. I couldn't bear the trauma of more broken butterflies in one day." Frank mercifully consented to go to the store for more glasses.

While he was gone, I sat staring at the broken glasses a long time. Then I threw them in the trash. After all, there's no need to cry over broken butterflies even if you can't get them home before the break.

Sometimes broken dreams also need to be discarded for fresh ones. For years an unquenchable ambition kept me striving for bigger and better attainments. I continually felt unfulfilled, pinched, even worthless.

One year I started a journal. On the first page I included a list of the things I wanted to obtain. They were goals. Even though clothed with spirituality, ambition was the body of their content.

One afternoon last year, I was walking home from a neighbor's house wallowing in new, unbridled ambitious fantasies.

Like a piercing shot, God interrupted my thoughts. "Linda," He spoke to my heart in an inner voice, "remember your list of goals you made several years ago."

"Oh, yes, Lord."

"I've given you every one of those things on your list and you still aren't satisfied," the Lord reminded me. Then with a final pierce the Lord said, "Seek me. Obtaining ambitious goals only leads to more consuming ambition."

For the first time in a number of years I could smile in satisfaction. God took the ambition and buried it. I realized I had been fighting a mounting snowball of fleshly attainments. It seemed that the more I was able to do, the more things I saw which I wanted to do but couldn't. One goal reached only meant that five more loomed illusively in the foreground taunting and hassling me. I saw again there is only one attainment which fully satisfies. "I want more of Jesus, so I'll give him more of me." That's satisfaction.

Broken butterflies and broken dreams shouldn't be held onto and cherished. They should be thrown away with the other trash.

43

Either We Have a God or We Don't

Leah's breathing thickened. The word, "asthma," ran through my aching heart like ice. Even though it was the middle of the night, I had diagnosed Leah's problem from all the signs I saw by her labored breath.

Fear was ruling my spirit. Hadn't I read only a few days ago that asthma was the seventh leading killer in the United States? Hadn't I heard that asthma was a demon? Wasn't it caused from emotional disturbances? What will my friends think? Doesn't asthma develop because a child is disturbed and nervous?

A thousand tormenting thoughts whirled through my brain. Frank and I had both prayed. Still the wheeze slowly crept into Leah's lungs.

I slipped into our bed and nudged myself close to Frank. "Honey, please pray for Leah."

"I did pray for her."

"Well, pray again. She's getting worse."

"No," Frank said as he slipped his arm around my waist

and drew me closer to him. "I prayed once. God heard me."

I couldn't hold the tears another minute.

Frank spoke softly, "Either we have a God or we don't have one. We can trust Him. It's that simple."

"Well, I want Him to do something now."

The next morning as I took Leah to the doctor, Frank's words and tender firmness were still ringing in my heart.

"Leah's problem is bronchitis," the doctor said after a close examination. "A shot and some medication will fix her right up." A smile and a pat on Leah's cheek reassured both of us.

We drove home. My relief knew no bounds. Bronchitis, not asthma! I didn't remember bronchitis even being on the "Top Ten Killers" list.

Settling back in my favorite chair at home, I prayed, "What do you want me to learn from all this, Lord?"

Softly I heard Frank's warm, night voice, "Either we have a God or we don't."

Can I depend on God? Not now that it's day and circumstances are comfortable. What about in the middle of the night when Satan bombards me with accusations? Am I willing to walk in new and even hard plains with Jesus? Do I want Him more than reputation, more than life?

Many times I have had to ask myself that same question. Now as always there was only one answer, "Yes."

The pain, heartaches, frustration of life will come, but we don't have to go through the night accusations alone. We have Jesus.

Before I went into the kitchen to start supper, I checked Leah. Her breathing was fine.

44

The 700 Club Mania

There is an enveloping, absorbing mania which is sweeping through the Christian community of our small town like an epidemic. It's the 700 Club.

The 700 Club is a Christian talk show starring Pat Robertson and his guests. They are all well-known Christian personalities. It is a professional production which skillfully incorporates teaching, miracles, healing, salvation and humor. About seven months ago it started showing on a local television station. The results have been phenomenal.

You just aren't quite with it unless you watch the 700 Club every day. Missing a week of shows means only one thing. You must have lost your salvation.

At first I strongly resisted this gripping, growing hysteria. I refused to watch even one show. Believe me, it was hard. Daily I would get a phone call from someone asking, "Are you watching the 700 Club?"

"No," I always rather piously replied. "I know it's wonderful, but I just don't have the time to spend watching television. I'm much too busy with the Lord's work." That usually meant I was cleaning out the bathroom.

About a month ago, I decided that I would watch the 700 Club each morning for one week. I planned my days to include it.

I can understand why I got all those phone calls. Now, I'm planning all my days not around my husband, the children, my work, but the 700 Club.

It comes on at nine-thirty in the morning. I hurry to finish my housework early. Then I sit my four-year-old daughter down with ninety-five assorted toys, puzzles and games so she can amuse herself. I put a DO NOT DISTURB sign on the door, close all the windows and curtains, turn on the television and settle down for an hour and a half of joy. The whole world comes to a screeching halt until eleven o'clock when the last prayer is prayed.

The other day I was completely enthralled in the 700 Club when I got a call from the church prayer chain.

"Pray for the Calvary Baptist Church." I vaguely remember a voice giving the request. "The woods around the church building have caught on fire. There is fire completely surrounding it. Pray that the church won't catch on fire also."

I quickly scrawled something down and went back to Pat and his special guest. At eleven when the 700 Club faded, I reread the prayer request. "Oh, my," I was startled to read the message I had scribbled. "Calvary Baptist Church has burned down."

I hurried to call all my friends with this urgent prayer need. "Calvary Baptist Church has burned down," I fervently passed the word to friend and enemy alike. "We must pray for them."

It wasn't until later that afternoon I found out that I had gotten the message messed up. I spent the next hours calling all the people I had contacted. I had to tell friend and enemy alike that I was wrong.

I probably should go back to my old resolve and quit watching Pat. But I know I can't now. Watching daily miracles is too exciting. I guess there's only one other solution. I have to remember to take the phone off the hook.

45

Out of the Concrete Box

My first encounter with a "concrete box housewife" was about eleven years ago. At that time I had been a full-time homemaker for only two years.

Carol worked hard to keep her house clean. One day as we sat over a cup of coffee, she said, "When Robert comes home, I take him for a tour of the house. I show him all the work I've done. I tell him how I cleaned the commode and about how hard it was to get the stain out of his collar."

I was shocked. How could any woman justify such trivia? When a man comes home from work, the last thing he wants is a running account of laundry and bathrooms. Being fresh from the business world, I could remember coming home tired and worn from a hard day. I certainly didn't want someone to stick my nose in a bathroom sink to show me how it sparkled.

One thing disturbed me the most about Carol's attitude. I knew she was desperately trying to justify her worth to her husband. I quietly prayed the Lord would give Carol a new sense of worth and self-satisfaction.

Thirteen years have passed since my last job as a secretary. One day I became appalled at myself as I realized I was rehearsing the speech I would give Frank when he came home from work. "Dear," I thought, "I cleaned both bathrooms today. The baby made the most awful mess on the kitchen floor. It took me almost an hour to clean it up. . . ."

Interrupting my speech, I prayed, "Lord, I've fallen into the same trap so many other housewives have."

I had built a concrete box of self-pity. The sense of my own worth was lost. All the satisfaction I once had, had been worn away by dirty diapers and unmade beds. Trying to justify to my husband my job and responsibilities, I made elaborate speeches about the fine job I was doing.

Suddenly I detested myself. I detested my husband. Even worse, there seemed no other way for me. My children and Frank do need me at home.

As I peeked over the sides of my concrete box I found the Lord's helping hand extended toward me. That day I slowly began the hard struggle out of the box which I had constructed from my duties in our home.

Soon after that, I was studying the chapter in the Bible which describes God's ideal woman, Proverbs 31. Verse 24 stuck out like a neon light. It says, "She maketh fine linen, and selleth it; and delivereth girdles unto the merchant." God's woman allowed herself the leeway to earn some of her own money.

For the most part, women with small children should stay at home. However, this woman had a money-making job which centered around the home. My situation doesn't merit working outside; yet I had begun to feel like a parasite. It didn't seem to matter that my husband makes a good salary.

Maybe this was the Holy Spirit's prodding, for it's not God's plan to produce parasites. Looking at the example of friends and relatives, I realized that with imagination and persistence paid work can be done in the home. I saw Christian friends who were making contributions to their households by selling cosmetics or giving piano lessons, etc. One neighbor gets most of her new furniture by holding two garage sales each year.

I began writing. It became an interesting outlet. Until then I had never allowed myself to receive money for anything I did. I felt everything had to be given away. Now I see it's part of God's plan for my life to sell my fine linen to the merchants.

Verse 16 of Chapter 31 was another eye widener. "She considereth a field, and buyeth it: with the fruit of her hands she planteth a vineyard."

Honestly, I have never wanted to plant or have a vineyard. Yet I did have a secret longing—to play the piano. In order to play the way I wanted, it would take time, energy and money.

My piano lessons started again but I found I had to take a realistic approach to them. Accomplished pianists aren't made after only a year or two of lessons. It would take maybe ten years. So I decided to give myself ten years of lessons. If I don't play the way I want to at the end of ten years, then I'll allow myself another ten years!

Each of us has fields we have been considering. They are secret gems held close to our hearts, secret desires. God gives us an example in the Proverbs woman. Become like her. Buy that field (anything worth having always costs something) and begin to plant it.

The greatest discovery and a giant step out of my concrete box of self-pity came about a year ago. While attending a

Bible study the question of housework came up. "How do you get to like housework?" one of the women asked.

"Yeah, how can anyone come to enjoy that mundane, never ending job?" The sarcasm dripped from my voice. Because I had left my house a complete wreck that day, I was particularly aggravated. It was going to take a steam shovel to haul all the mess out.

The teacher smiled. She laid her pencil down and quietly folded her hands. "When you find out who you are in Christ Jesus," she said, "you won't have to worry about what your job is. It isn't the job which makes the person. It's the person who makes the job. Isn't that the most fundamental part of Christian living?"

My face turned red with shame. For years I had taught and harped on knowing who you are in Jesus. Didn't I know that principle? Why hadn't I been able to put it into practice?

When I came home from the meeting, I pulled off my coat and dropped it. I fell to my knees and wept. "Lord, I have forgotten who I am in you. Maybe I never did know. I desperately need you to change my attitude. Teach me what it means to be a child of God."

When I got up from my knees, I didn't feel different but I knew God had heard my prayer. Since that day, I've experienced the joy of being a child of the King even when I'm cleaning up spilled milk or sweeping the floor.

The Lord taught me to transfer the realistic approach I had taken with my piano lessons to my housework. I had been too idealistic. I can't do everything. Some things will have to be left until another day. I can only do one thing at a time. I am to enjoy what I'm doing because of who I am, not because the job is important.

Each household job can become a secret mission in which

the Lord is molding me into his image. Cleaning the woodwork on my knees is an act of surrender to my heavenly Father, not a demeaning, humiliating task. Things don't always get done on time but I'm learning. When I'm late or do something wrong, I take the blame. Say I'm sorry. Then I go on to do the other things which have to be done. I'm learning not to take on condemnation.

What joy it has become to see Jesus turn my self-pity into self-worth and satisfaction. How comforting it is to see that concrete box I erected being turned back into a home.

EPILOGUE

A Visiting Dove

I gently scooped the injured mourning dove into both hands and put him on the edge of the big white planter in the living room.

His large innocent eyes searched each move I made. He stayed there several days eating from my hands, perched on the planter or on my finger.

His trusting gentleness was overwhelming. In a few hours, he seemed completely tame and would willingly step onto my finger.

As I walked from the kitchen into the living room after supper, his eyes caught mine. I stared at the lovely bird for a long time. "What if this dove were the Holy Spirit come to visit our home," I thought.

"Oh, my actions and reactions would certainly be different," came the quick reply to my own question.

I glanced at the brown bird again. Quietly from the depth of my spirit came a loving coo. "I haven't come for a visit, Linda. I live here every day."

For free information on how to receive
the international magazine

LOGOS JOURNAL

also Book Catalog

Write: Information - LOGOS JOURNAL CATALOG
Box 191
Plainfield, NJ 07061